TOFU
Cookery

by Louise Hagler

The Book Publishing Company • Summertown, Tennessee 38483

Editor:
Louise Hagler

Managing Editor:
Jane Ayers

Recipe-Testing Coordinator:
Colleen Pride

Nutritional Consultant:
Margaret Nofziger

Food Stylists:
Jane Ayers
Louise Hagler

Photographer:
Michael Bonnickson

Art:
Peter Hoyt
Gregory Lowry

ACKNOWLEDGEMENTS

Our special thanks go to the following people from The Farm in Summertown, Tennessee, for originating and developing the recipes in this book: Dorothy Bates, Stewart Butler, Mary Felber, Claire Fitch, Louise Hagler, Nancy Haren, Sarah Hergenrather, Dawn Huddleston, Jane Hunnicutt, Sylvia Hupp, Suzy Jenkins, Roberta Kachinsky, Betsy Keller, Beth Kramer, Lani Lichtman, Marian Lyon, Kathryn McClure, Earlynn McIntyre, Cornelia Mandelstein, Lee Meltzer, Ann Moore, Stacey Moore, Laurie Praskin, Carol Pratt, Colleen Pride, Rachel Sythe, Honey Tepper, Ruth Thomas.

Thanks to James Egan, Leon Fainbuch and John Pielaszczyk for layout and typography.

Cover Photo: Enchiladas (page 66); Honey Cheesecake with Kiwis and Blueberries (page 139); and Almond Salad (page 29).

ISBN 0-913990-38-8

Table of Contents

Introducing Tofu

Tofu is one of the most versatile protein foods in the world. It has been a protein staple in parts of Asia for over 2,000 years and is now becoming a household word in the West. Tofu, also known as *bean curd*, is made by curding the mild white "milk" of the soybean. It is high in protein and low in calories, fats, and carbohydrates. Tofu is an economical source of protein, and contains no cholesterol.

Tofu can be prepared in any number of delicious ways. The recipes in this book are only a sampling of the culinary delights possible with tofu, ranging from the familiar to the international and exotic. Tofu can be prepared in a variety of main dishes, breads, desserts, soups, salads, salad dressings, and dips for any meal, snack, or party.

With its growing popularity, tofu has become easy to find in supermarkets everywhere, usually in the produce section along with oriental vegetables. It can also be found in many oriental food shops and health food stores. Tofu shops and plants are also sprouting up around the country; if you become a serious tofu chef or use large amounts of tofu, you might want to make arrangements to get it right from the source. Or you can make your own tofu at home. (See directions on page 155.)

Tofu is also an excellent food for babies, children, and the elderly, because it is a wholesome, complete vegetable protein that is very easy to digest. It is a good food for sensitive stomachs. For babies, tofu can be blended in the blender or ground in a baby food grinder with whatever flavoring, fruit, or vegetable you like.

For dairy-free cooking, use soymilk in the recipes which call for either milk or soymilk. (Directions for making soymilk are included on page 155.) Each recipe has a nutritional analysis, giving the amount per serving of calories, protein, fat, and carbohydrates.

As you gain experience using tofu, you can adapt many of your own favorite recipes to include it. Tofu fits easily as a low calorie dressing, whip, or dip; as an inexpensive alternative to meat, fish, poultry, or cheese; or as a protein extender in baked goods. There is a whole new world of cooking and eating awaiting you using this nutritious, multifaceted food from the East. Happy cooking and eating!

Spaghetti Primavera

GETTING TO KNOW YOUR TOFU

Buying and Handling Tofu

Tofu can be made or bought in several different forms. These range from silken tofu, which is the softest form, to a medium soft Japanese-style, to a medium firm Chinese-style, to hard pressed tofu, which is a very dense and firm cheese. There are many forms available in between, depending on how the tofu was made.

Fresh tofu has a fresh and delicate scent to it. This is tofu at its best. It barely has any smell at all when really fresh. Each package of tofu should show an expiration date. Be sure to check for this when buying tofu.

If fresh tofu is handled right, it can keep for up to one week in your refrigerator. It should be kept submerged in cold water, and the water should be changed daily to keep it fresh and moist.

The firmer types of tofu are best used for slicing or cubing and sometimes crumbling. The softer tofu can be used for slicing and cubing also, but it does not hold its shape well if it is handled a lot. The softer kinds of tofu are best for blending, mashing, and crumbling.

If you want a firm tofu and you can only find soft, you can slice the tofu into slabs, place the slabs side by side between towels, and set another towel and a heavy breadboard or other similar weight on it for 20 to 30 minutes.

If the tofu you buy smells a little sour, it is still usable, but it is best to boil it for about twenty minutes, which will change its texture

Tofu Blocks

somewhat, making it harder and chewier. We do not recommend using tofu in this state for blending in a blender or for use in any dessert or fresh salad or dip. If the tofu you buy smells very sour, we suggest that you return it to your grocer for a replacement and recommend that he keep it at a cooler temperature.

Measuring Tofu

There are a couple of ways to measure tofu when it is not pre-measured for you in a package. If you are going to slice or cube the tofu, use the water displacement method. Fill a 4-cup measuring cup with 3 cups water. Then float a block of tofu that brings the water level up to the 4-cup level. This will give you 1/2 lb. of tofu.

You may have to take a slice off the block if the water level rises above the 4-cup mark. If the water doesn't reach the 4-cup level when you put the block in, add a slice or two until the water level comes up to 4 cups. Be sure to check at eye level when measuring, and don't press the tofu down under the water. If you are going to blend, mash, or crumble the tofu, you can measure it in a measuring cup in the mashed or crumbled form. One cup is equal to 1/2 lb. of tofu.

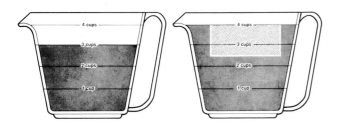

Displacement Method of Measuring Tofu

Blending Tofu

When you are blending tofu, there are a few points to remember. Blend it as you would any dense material and don't try to do too much at a time. In a standard home blender, it is a good rule to blend no more than 1/2 lb. at a time, but this could vary with different types of blenders and the softness of the tofu. It will help to mash or crumble your tofu before blending if it is not very soft.

Unless the tofu is quite soft, you will not be able to put everything in the blender, turn it on and leave it to blend. It will probably need to be coaxed from the sides gently with a rubber spatula to keep it circulating. Be careful not to touch the blades with the spatula. If you don't have a blender, an electric mixer works well on the softer tofu. A food processor will also work, but generally does not make as creamy a finished product as a blender.

If a recipe calls for more than 1/2 lb. of tofu to be blended in a blender along with other ingredients, you can break up the tofu in a bowl and add the other ingredients. Then, stir it all up and divide the mixture into smaller batches to blend. Use only about 1/2 lb. of tofu per batch. Then, put it all together again in a bowl and stir well.

Frozen Tofu

Freezing tofu drastically changes its properties, and transforms it into a unique protein food. When you freeze it, thaw it, and squeeze out the water, the tofu resembles a spongy latticework, which has a more meaty, chewy consistency than regular tofu. It soaks up marinades and sauces more readily than the plain form. Just drain it, wrap it in foil or plastic, and put it in the freezer until frozen into a solid block. You can let it thaw at room temperature or pour boiling water over it as needed. Frozen tofu adds yet more variety to an already versatile food.

Marinating

Tofu and marinades were meant for each other. Always marinate in glass, stainless steel, or enamel. Marinating slices or cubes of tofu works best in a flat pan. See Korean Barbecue, p. 81. The pieces should be carefully turned several times, or you can use a turkey baster to suck the marinade up and squirt it back over the pieces. With frozen tofu, you will need to mix and squeeze the marinade into the tofu. When a recipe calls for marinating tofu for one hour or less, it can be done at room temperature covered with wax paper or a towel. For longer periods of time, marinating should be done in a tightly covered container in the refrigerator because of the risk of bacterial growth.

Dips and Spreads

Clockwise from top left: Pimento Dip or Spread, Walnut Olive Dip, and Parsley-Onion Dip

---

DIPS AND SPREADS

A medium soft tofu or Japanese-style tofu is the best for dips. Dips are creamiest when made in a blender, but can also be made with a food processor or electric mixer. Read "Blending Tofu" on p. 7. Use very fresh tofu for making dips. For lower calorie dips and spreads, you can leave out the oil. Most dips taste best if you make them ahead of time and let them sit in the refrigerator for several hours to fully develop the flavors.

Dry Onion Soup Dip

Makes 2 3/4 cups

This is the classic California dip made with tofu.

Have ready:
2 1/2 cups of Tofu Sour Creme Dressing (double recipe, omitting salt), p. 41

Stir or blend in:
1 pkg. (scant 1/2 cup) dry onion soup mix

It's best if refrigerated for about 4 hours to overnight.

Per Serving: Calories: 127, Protein: 3 gm., Fat: 12 gm., Carbohydrates: 4 gm.

Onion Dip

Makes 1 1/2 cups

Have ready:
1 1/4 cups Tofu Sour Creme Dressing, p. 41

Stir into dressing:
1/3 cup dried onions, minced
1 Tbsp. vegetable bouillon granules
1 1/4 tsp. garlic powder
1 tsp. onion powder

Refrigerate at least 4 hours before serving.

Per 1/4 Cup Serving: Calories: 113, Protein: 3 gm., Fat: 10 gm., Carbohydrates: 2 gm.

Walnut-Olive Dip

Makes 1 3/4 cups

Blend in a blender until smooth and creamy:

1/2 lb. tofu, mashed   **3 Tbsp. fresh lemon juice**
2 Tbsp. oil   **1/2 tsp. salt**
2 tsp. sugar

Fold in:

2 Tbsp. walnuts, finely chopped
4 tsp. black olives, chopped

Per 1/4 Cup Serving: Calories: 75, Protein: 3 gm., Fat: 6 gm., Carbohydrates: 3 gm.

Chive Dip

Makes 2 1/2 cups

Blend in a blender until smooth and creamy:

1 lb. tofu   **1 Tbsp. soy sauce**
1/3 cup oil   **1/2 tsp. garlic powder**
1 Tbsp. vinegar   **1/4 tsp. black pepper**

Pour into a bowl, then fold in:
1/2 cup fresh chives, chopped

Per 1/4 Cup Serving: Calories: 99, Protein: 4 gm., Fat: 9 gm., Carbohydrates: 1 gm.

Pimento Dip or Spread

Makes 2 1/4 cups

Good for sandwich filling, on crackers or as a dip.

Blend in a blender until smooth and creamy:

1/2 cup tofu   **1 1/2 tsp. salt**
2 Tbsp. oil   **pinch garlic powder**
2 Tbsp. apple cider vinegar   **1/8 tsp. black pepper**
1 Tbsp. sugar

Pour into a bowl and mix in:
1 lb. tofu, crumbled
3 Tbsp. sweet pickle relish
1/2 cup pimentos, chopped

This is best if refrigerated overnight.

Per 1/4 Cup Serving: Calories: 86, Protein: 5 gm., Fat: 5 gm., Carbohydrates: 5 gm.

Honolulu Dip

Makes 2 cups

Blend in a blender until smooth and creamy:

1 1/3 cups tofu, mashed	1/2 tsp. prepared mustard
5 Tbsp. ketchup	1/2 tsp. prepared horseradish
1/4 cup vinegar	scant 1/8 tsp.: ginger
1/4 cup oil	cayenne
4 tsp. soy sauce	garlic powder
2 tsp. peanut butter	cinnamon
1 tsp. honey	

Per 1/4 Cup Serving: Calories: 109, Protein: 3 gm., Fat: 9 gm., Carbohydrates: 5 gm.

Dill Dip

Makes 1 1/4 cups

Blend in a blender until smooth and creamy:

3/4 cup tofu, mashed	1 1/2 tsp. sugar
2 Tbsp. oil	1 tsp. dill weed
2 1/2 Tbsp. wine vinegar	1/8 tsp. black pepper
1 tsp. salt	1 Tbsp. onion, minced

Per 1/4 Cup Serving: Calories: 72, Protein: 3 gm., Fat: 7 gm., Carbohydrates: 1 gm.

Almond Dip

Makes 1 1/2 cups

Blend in a blender until smooth and creamy:

1/2 lb. tofu, mashed	2 tsp. sugar
3 Tbsp. fresh lemon juice	1/2 tsp. salt
2 Tbsp. oil	

Fold in:
1/4 cup roasted slivered almonds

Per 1/4 Cup Serving: Calories: 101, Protein: 4 gm., Fat: 9 gm., Carbohydrates: 4 gm.

Caper Spread

Makes 1 1/2 cups

Blend in blender until smooth and creamy:
1/2 lb. tofu   **1/2 tsp. salt**
2 Tbsp. oil   **1 tsp. dijon mustard**
2 Tbsp. caper juice

Pour this into a bowl which has been rubbed with:
1 clove garlic, cut in half

Fold in:
1 Tbsp. onion, finely minced
1 Tbsp. capers (large ones, cut in half)

Per 1/4 Cup Serving: Calories: 69, Protein: 3 gm., Fat: 6 gm., Carbohydrates: 1 gm.

Sweet and Sour Curry Dip

Makes 1 3/4 cups

This is a good dip for raw vegetables.

Blend in a blender until smooth and creamy:
1/2 lb. tofu, mashed   **1 Tbsp. curry powder**
1/4 cup oil   **1 1/2 Tbsp. soy sauce**
1/2 cup brown sugar   **1 Tbsp. vinegar**
1/4 cup mustard

Per 1/4 Cup Serving: Calories: 161, Protein: 3 gm., Fat: 9 gm., Carbohydrates: 23 gm.

Curry Dip

Makes 1 1/4 cups

Good with raw vegetables.

Blend in a blender until smooth and creamy:
1/2 cup tofu, crumbled   **1 1/2 tsp. curry powder (more if you like)**
1/4 cup oil   **1/2 tsp. sugar**
2 Tbsp. vinegar   **1/2 tsp. garlic powder**
3/4 tsp. salt

Chill.

Per 1/4 Cup Serving: Calories: 115, Protein: 2 gm., Fat: 12 gm., Carbohydrates: 1 gm.

Guacamole Dip

Mash or blend in a blender:
2 ripe avocados (about 1 1/2 cups)

Stir in:
3/4 cup tomato, chopped
1/2 cup Tofu Salad Dressing, p. 42
1/4 cup green taco sauce
2 tsp. onion powder or
1/4 cup finely chopped onions

1 tsp. garlic powder or
3 cloves garlic, pressed
1/2 tsp. salt

Per 1/4 Cup Serving: Calories: 132, Protein: 2 gm., Fat: 12 gm., Carbohydrates: 5 gm.

Jalapeno Dip

This dip is for folks who like it "hot"!

Blend in a blender until smooth and creamy:
3/4 lb. tofu
1/4 cup oil
1 pickled jalapeno pepper,
more or less to taste

1/2 small onion, chopped
2 Tbsp. fresh parsley
1/2 tsp. salt

Chill for 2 hours before serving.

This dip is hot by American standards and gets hotter after it has been chilled.

Per 1/4 Cup Serving: Calories: 106, Protein: 4 gm., Fat: 10 gm., Carbohydrates: 1 gm.

Garlic Dip

Blend in a blender until smooth and creamy:
1/2 lb. tofu
1/4 cup oil
2 Tbsp. fresh lemon juice

1 Tbsp. sugar or honey
3/4 tsp. salt
3 cloves garlic

Stir in:
1 clove garlic, minced fine

Per 1/4 Cup Serving: Calories: 119, Protein: 3 gm., Fat: 11 gm., Carbohydrates: 4 gm.

Parsley-Onion Dip

Blend in a blender until smooth and creamy:

1 lb. tofu, mashed

1/2 cup fresh parsley leaves

1 small red onion, chopped (1/3 cup) or

  2 tsp. onion powder

2-4 Tbsp. oil

2 Tbsp. fresh lemon juice

1 tsp. salt

Per 1/4 Cup Serving: Calories: 56, Protein: 3 gm., Fat: 4 gm., Carbohydrates: 2 gm.

Tofu and Green Bean Spread

Mash together well:

1 cup cut green beans, cooked and drained

3/4 cup tofu

1/2 cup boiled potatoes

Saute together:

1/4 cup oil

1 large onion, chopped

Add:

3/4 tsp. soy sauce

1/2 tsp. salt

1/4 tsp. onion salt

Mix everything together and add:

1 small onion, chopped fine

2 Tbsp. ground roasted sunflower seeds

(these can be ground in the blender)

Garnish with paprika and parsley and serve.

Per 1/4 Cup Serving: Calories: 173, Protein: 5 gm., Fat: 14 gm., Carbohydrates: 8 gm.

Soups

Zucchini Bisque and Basic Fried Tofu sandwich

SOUPS

Zucchini Bisque

Makes 6 cups

Saute:
1/4 cup oil
1 medium onion, chopped
1 1/2 lbs. zucchini, sliced
2 tsp. salt

Add to the sauteed vegetables, cover and simmer 20 minutes:
2 1/2 cups stock or water
1/2 tsp. nutmeg
1/8 tsp. freshly ground black pepper

Remove from heat and let cool 5 minutes.

Blend in a blender until smooth and creamy:
1/2 lb. tofu
2 Tbsp. oil

Stir blended tofu mixture into sauteed vegetables. Heat, but do not boil. Garnish with "Smoky Tofu Bits," p. 29, and serve.

Per 1 Cup Serving: Calories: 164, Protein: 4 gm., Fat: 15 gm., Carbohydrates: 5 gm.

Brothy Soup

Makes 2 quarts

Freeze, thaw, squeeze out, and cut in 3/4" cubes:
1/2 lb. tofu

Marinate for 1 hour in a mixture of:
2 Tbsp. soy sauce
1/4 tsp. garlic powder

Saute the marinated tofu in:
1 1/2 Tbsp. oil

When lightly browned, remove from heat. Set aside.

Slice into 1/4" pieces:
3 small carrots
3 small potatoes
1 medium onion
1/2 cup fresh parsley

Bring to boil:
5 cups water
1 Tbsp. vegetable bouillon

Add vegetables and simmer 20 minutes or until the vegetables are tender. Add browned tofu. Serve hot.

Per 1 Cup Serving: Calories: 68, Protein: 3 gm., Fat: 4 gm., Carbohydrates: 6 gm.

Minestrone Soup

Makes 11 cups

Freeze, thaw, squeeze out and cut into 3/4″ cubes:
1 lb. tofu

Preheat oven to 375° F.

Mix together:
3 Tbsp. soy sauce
1/2 tsp. garlic powder

Mix and squeeze this mixture into the tofu cubes. Then bake the cubes on an oiled cookie sheet for 10 minutes. Turn the cubes and bake 5 minutes more. Set aside.

Saute together for about 10 minutes:
2 Tbsp. olive oil
1 medium onion, chopped
1 stalk celery, chopped
2 carrots, sliced
1 medium zucchini, sliced

Combine the sauteed vegetables in a soup pot with:
1 (28 oz.) can tomatoes, chopped
2 cups tomato juice
4 cups water
1/2 tsp. garlic powder
1 tsp. oregano
2 tsp. basil
1/4 tsp. pepper
1/2 tsp. salt

Bring to a boil and add:
3 oz. noodles or broken spaghetti

Simmer for 15 minutes, then add:
1 (15 oz.) can kidney beans
the browned tofu cubes

Serve when beans and tofu are heated through.

Per 1 Cup Serving: Calories: 167, Protein: 8 gm., Fat: 7 gm., Carbohydrates: 18 gm.

Curried Tofu-Apple Soup

Makes 3 quarts

A mild curried soup.

Freeze, thaw, squeeze dry and cut or tear into bite-size pieces:
1 1/2 lbs. tofu

Wash, pare and dice:
4-5 apples

Heat to boiling:
2 qts. stock or water

Add apples and boil 2 minutes, then set aside, reserving liquid.

In another pan, saute together:
1/2 cup oil
1/2 cup onions, chopped

When onions are almost transparent, add tofu and lightly fry.

While they are frying, sprinkle with:
1/3 cup unbleached white flour
2 Tbsp. curry powder
2 tsp. salt

Stir well, then add:
2 cups water from the apple cooking pot

Stir constantly to avoid making lumps. Then pour it back into the apple cooking pot, stir, cover and simmer 10-15 minutes. Serve.

Per 1 Cup Serving: Calories: 157, Protein: 5 gm., Fat: 11 gm., Carbohydrates: 10 gm.

Tofu Chowder

Makes 2 quarts

Saute together for 15 minutes in a 4-6 quart pot:
2 Tbsp. oil   **2 carrots, chopped**
1 medium onion, chopped   **3 celery stalks, chopped**

Pour in:
2 cups water
2 cups milk or soymilk

Add:
1/2 lb. tofu, crumbled   **1/2 tsp. black pepper**
2 tsp. salt   **1/2 tsp. celery seed**

Bring to a boil and add:
2 large potatoes,
peeled and cubed (about 2 cups)

Simmer until potatoes are soft. Serve.

Per 1 Cup Serving: Calories: 130, Protein: 6 gm., Fat: 7 gm., Carbohydrates: 13 gm.

Mulligatawny Soup

Makes 2 quarts

Freeze, thaw, squeeze dry and cut into 1/2" cubes:
  1/2 lb. tofu

Saute in a dutch oven or large saucepan:
  1/4 cup oil   **1 carrot, sliced**
  1/2 cup onion, chopped   **1 1/2 cups celery, chopped**

When onion is soft, sprinkle over and stir in:
  1 1/2 Tbsp. unbleached white flour
  2 tsp. curry powder

Simmer for 3 minutes, then stir in:
  2 cups water or vegetable bouillon   **1/3 cup apple, chopped**
  the tofu cubes   **1 1/2 tsp. salt**
  1 cup stewed tomatoes, chopped   **1/4 tsp. black pepper**

Simmer 15 minutes, then add:
  1/2 cup milk or soymilk

Serve immediately.

Per 1 Cup Serving: Calories: 116, Protein: 4 gm., Fat: 9 gm., Carbohydrates: 7 gm.

Lentil Soup

Serves 6

Wash and drain:
  1 cup lentils

Bring to a boil in a large pot with:
  1 qt. water
  1/2 tsp. salt

In a skillet, saute together:
  2 Tbsp. oil   **1 medium carrot, sliced**
  1 medium onion, diced   **1 celery stalk, sliced**
  1 clove garlic, minced

When onion is soft, add all to boiling lentils with:
  1 cup peeled tomatoes or
  1/2 (6 oz.) can tomato paste

Simmer for another 30 minutes.

Add:
  1/2 lb. tofu, cut in small cubes   **1/4 tsp. basil**
  1 1/2 tsp. wine vinegar   **1/8 tsp. black pepper**

Continue simmering until lentils are soft. Serve.

Per 1 Cup Serving: Calories: 195, Protein: 12 gm., Fat: 6 gm., Carbohydrates: 25 gm.

Watercress or Bok Choy Soup

Makes 2 1/2 quarts

Bring to a boil:
2 qts. water

Add and dissolve:
1 cube vegetable bouillon
1 Tbsp. salt

Add:
1 lb. tofu, cut in 1 1/2" x 1/4" x 1/4" pieces
1 small onion, diced

Simmer 10-15 minutes, then add:
1 bunch watercress, coarsely chopped

Cook 3 more minutes, then serve immediately.

Variation: Add about 25 Won Tons (see p. 93) in the last 5 minutes of cooking or 4 oz. flat noodles along with onion and tofu.

Variation: For Bok Choy Soup, chop 1/2 lb. bok choy diagonally every 1/2" and separate into stem and leaf pieces. Add stem pieces 4-5 minutes before serving. Add leaf pieces 3 minutes before serving.

Per Serving: Calories: 36, Protein: 4 gm., Fat: 2 gm., Carbohydrates: 2 gm.

Miso Soup

Serves 6

Miso is a salty, cultured bean paste from which soy sauce evolved. It can be found in the oriental food section of a supermarket or in a health food store.

Saute together in a soup pot until limp but not brown:
1/4 cup oil   **4-6 carrots, sliced**
1 small head cabbage, shredded   **3 stalks celery, sliced**
3-4 small onions, diced

Add:
2 qts. hot water   **1/4 tsp. black pepper**
1 tsp. salt

Simmer 30 minutes.

Cut into 3/4" cubes and add to the soup:
1 lb. tofu

Dissolve together:
1/2 cup cold water
1/4 cup miso

Stir into soup. Heat but do not boil. Serve when tofu is heated through.

Per 1 Cup Serving: Calories: 98, Protein: 5 gm., Fat: 6 gm., Carbohydrates: 7 gm.

Watercress Soup with Won Ton

Hot and Sour Soup

Makes 6 cups

Bring to a boil:
  4 cups water

Add:
  1/2 lb. tofu, slivered
  2 cups cabbage, thinly sliced
  2 vegetable bouillon cubes

  3/4 tsp. salt
  1 Tbsp. soy sauce

Simmer together for 3 minutes.

Add:
  2 Tbsp. white vinegar
  1/4 tsp. cayenne

Bring back to a boil.

Dissolve together:
  3 Tbsp. water
  2 Tbsp. cornstarch

Stir the dissolved mixture into the soup. Serve garnished with chopped green onions and 2 teaspoons Chinese sesame seed oil (optional).

Per 1 Cup Serving: Calories: 51, Protein: 4 gm., Fat: 2 gm., Carbohydrates: 5 gm.

Lemon Soup

Makes 2 1/2 quarts

Have ready:
  1/2 cup cooked rice

Bring to a boil:
  5 cups water

Add:
  1 lb. firm tofu, slivered 1/8" x 1" or 2" pieces
  2 vegetable bouillon cubes
  1 1/2 tsp. salt

Cover and simmer 10 minutes.

Add:
  2 cups milk or soymilk

Whisk together, then whisk into the soup pot:
  5 Tbsp. lemon juice
  2 Tbsp. cornstarch

Add:
  1/2 cup cooked rice

Cook, without boiling, until slightly thickened. Serve hot or cold garnished with chopped parsley and a thin slice of lemon.

Per 1 Cup Serving: Calories: 83, Protein: 6 gm., Fat: 4 gm., Carbohydrates: 8 gm.

Cream of Celery Soup

Makes 9 cups

Have ready:
  2 lbs. celery, coarsely chopped
  1 lb. green onions or leeks, coarsely chopped
  2 carrots, diced in 1/4" squares

Set these aside.

Combine in a 4 quart saucepan:
  1/4 cup oil
  3 Tbsp. unbleached white flour

Let these bubble together over low heat for about 2 minutes.

Whisk in:
  8 cups hot vegetable bouillon

Reserve 1 cup each of celery and carrots, then add the rest of the chopped vegetables to the thickened broth. Simmer for about 25 minutes or until the vegetables are tender.

Remove from heat and put it all through a food mill, or let it cool and blend in a blender until smooth.

While the vegetables are simmering in the thickened broth, saute until tender:
  2 Tbsp. oil
  the reserved celery pieces
  the reserved carrot pieces

Add the sauteed vegetables to the blended broth mixture along with:
  1 1/2 cups soft tofu, blended smooth and creamy
  1 tsp. salt
  1/2 tsp. freshly ground black pepper

If the soup needs to be reheated, do not let it boil. Serve immediately.

Per 1 Cup Serving: Calories: 149, Protein: 5 gm., Fat: 11 gm., Carbohydrates: 12 gm.

Salads

Greek Salad

SALADS

Greek Salad

Dressing

Mix together:
1/2 cup olive oil
1/4 cup wine vinegar
2 tsp. salt

1 tsp. basil
1/2 tsp. black pepper
1/2 tsp. oregano

Pour the dressing over:
1 lb. tofu, cut in 3/4" cubes

Marinate for at least 1 hour, stirring occasionally.

Wash, core and cut into wedges:
3 fresh tomatoes

Wash and slice thin:
3 cucumbers

Add these to the marinated tofu along with:
1/2 large red onion, chopped
1 cup Greek or black olives

Toss and serve on a bed of lettuce.

Per Serving: Calories: 252, Protein: 8 gm., Fat: 21 gm., Carbohydrates: 6 gm.

Spanish Tofu-Rice Salad

Marinate for 1/2 hour:
1/2 lb. tofu, cut in small cubes
1 tsp. salt

1/4 cup lemon juice
1/4 tsp. garlic powder

Mix together:
4 cups cooked rice
3 green onions, chopped
1/4 cup olive oil
1 green pepper, diced

1/4 cup lemon juice
2 tomatoes, diced
4 tsp. salt

Mix this together with marinated tofu. Chill for a few hours.

Mix in:
1/4-1/2 cup parsley, chopped
1/8 tsp. freshly ground black pepper

Serve.

Per Serving: Calories: 236, Protein: 5 gm., Fat: 9 gm., Carbohydrates: 33 gm.

Meal In A Bowl Salad

Mix together in a bowl:
- 1 qt. fresh salad greens
- 2 carrots, grated
- 1 celery stalk, minced
- 1/2 bell pepper, minced
- 2 small green onions, minced

Add to the salad:
- 1/2 lb. tofu, cubed and lightly sauteed in oil

Top the salad with 1/4 cup Garlic Dressing, below, and garnish with either 2 tablespoons "Smoky Tofu Bits," below, or purchased imitation bacon bits.

Garlic Dressing

Combine:
- 3 cloves garlic, crushed
- 6 Tbsp. oil
- 1/2 cup vinegar
- 1 cup water
- 3 Tbsp. sugar
- a pinch each of: salt, pepper, basil and celery seed

Shake together well before pouring. This makes more than enough for one salad, and the rest can be refrigerated for future use.

Smoky Tofu Bits

Makes 1/2 cup

Mix together in a frying pan:
- 1/2 lb. tofu, crumbled
- 1/4 cup soy sauce
- 1 clove garlic, crushed
- 1 Tbsp. sugar
- 1/2 tsp. ginger
- 1/4 tsp. black pepper
- 2 Tbsp. oil
- 2 Tbsp. water

Cook slowly until all moisture is gone and the tofu is brown and crunchy. Stir often so the bits don't burn.

Per Serving: Calories: 786, Protein: 31 gm., Fat: 56 gm., Carbohydrates: 45 gm.

Almond Salad

Serves 4-6
Makes 4 cups

Combine in a bowl:
- 1 1/2 lbs. tofu, cut in 1/2" cubes
- 3 Tbsp. fresh lemon juice
- 1/2 tsp. celery salt

Mix in:
- 1 1/2 cups celery, diced
- 1/3 cup green onion, minced
- 3/4 cup almonds, slivered and toasted
- 1/2 tsp. salt

Blend together with:
- 1 1/2 cups Tofu Sour Creme Dressing, p. 41

Chill and serve.

Per Serving: Calories: 371, Protein: 18 gm., Fat: 30 gm., Carbohydrates: 12 gm.

Tofu Pea Salad

Cut into 1/4″ cubes:
1 lb. tofu

Marinate the cubes for 1 hour in:
3 Tbsp. lemon juice

Drain tofu and reserve lemon juice.

Mix in a bowl:
4 green onions, chopped in 1/2″ pieces   **6 Tbsp. pimentos, chopped**
2 celery stalks, chopped in 1/2″ pieces

Add:
the drained tofu cubes
2 1/2 cups small fresh peas (you can substitute frozen or canned baby peas)

Dressing

Blend in a blender until smooth and creamy:
1/2 lb. tofu   **1 Tbsp. sugar**
3 Tbsp. oil   **1/2 tsp. salt**
3 Tbsp. reserved lemon juice

Stir the dressing into the salad and serve on a bed of lettuce.

Per Serving: Calories: 206, Protein: 15 gm., Fat: 12 gm., Carbohydrates: 4 gm.

Tofu Lentil Salad

Have ready:
2 cups cooked and drained lentils

Dressing

Mix together well:
1/4 cup oil   **1/2 tsp. salt**
2 Tbsp. vinegar   **1/4 tsp. black pepper**
1 tsp. curry powder

Salad

Mix together in a bowl:
3/4 lb. tofu, crumbled
the lentils

Stir in the dressing along with:
2 Tbsp. onion, diced   **1/4 cup sweet pickle relish**
1/2 cup celery, diced   **1 tsp. curry powder**
1/2 cup carrot, grated   **1 tsp. salt**

Chill and serve.

Per Serving: Calories: 433, Protein: 22 gm., Fat: 20 gm., Carbohydrates: 45 gm.

Potato Tofu Salad

Have ready:
 6 medium potatoes, cooked and peeled
 (about 6 cups cooked and cubed)

In large mixing bowl, put:
 1 cup tofu, crumbled
 the cooked, cubed potatoes
 1 cup celery, cut in 1/4" pieces

 1/2 cup red onion, chopped fine
 1/2 cup sweet pickle relish
 1 1/2 tsp. salt

Dressing

Blend in a blender until smooth and creamy:
 1 cup tofu
 1/4 cup oil
 1/2 tsp. salt
 1 1/2 Tbsp. cider vinegar

 1/2 Tbsp. lemon juice
 1/8 tsp. garlic powder
 dash black pepper
 1 Tbsp. salad mustard

Add dressing to the salad and mix gently. Chill and serve.

Per Serving: Calories: 236, Protein: 8 gm., Fat: 11 gm., Carbohydrates: 31 gm.

Picnic Potato Salad

Scrub well and cut up:
 4 medium potatoes

Boil in salted water until tender. Drain and pull skins off.

While still hot, toss with a mix of:
 2 Tbsp. oil
 1 Tbsp. vinegar
 1/2 tsp. salt

 1/8 tsp. black pepper
 1/8 tsp. dry mustard

Let cool. Add to the cooled potatoes:

 1/3 cup onion, minced
 1 cup celery, diced

 2 Tbsp. parsley, minced
 celery salt to taste

Dressing

Blend in a blender until smooth and creamy:
 3/4 cup tofu, mashed
 2 Tbsp. oil
 2 Tbsp. vinegar

Mix in dressing, chill and serve.

Per Serving: Calories: 265, Protein: 7 gm., Fat: 15 gm., Carbohydrates: 27 gm.

Molded Vegetable Salad

Serves 6
Makes one 4 1/2 cup mold

Soak for 5 minutes in a small saucepan:
- **3 cups water**
- **3 cubes vegetable bouillon**
- **.2 oz agar agar* or**
- **1/4 cup agar agar flakes***

After soaking, simmer for 15 minutes. Remove from heat.

Pour into a mixing bowl with:

- **1 cup celery, chopped fine**
- **3 Tbsp. onion, minced**
- **1 cup peas, fresh or frozen**
- **1/2 lb. tofu, blended**

- **1/4 cup sweet relish**
- **3 Tbsp. pimentos, chopped**
- **1/4 tsp. black pepper**

After mixing all ingredients thoroughly together, pour into the mold or individual serving dishes. Chill until firm (about 4-6 hours or overnight). Remove from mold and serve.

*Agar agar can be found in the special foods section of a supermarket or in a health food store. Regular gelatin can be substituted.

Per Serving: Calories: 70, Protein: 5 gm., Fat: 2 gm., Carbohydrates: 10 gm.

Molded Vegetable Salad

Molded Fruit and Vegetable Salad

Serves 6
Makes one 4 1/2 cup mold

Soak for 5 minutes in a small saucepan:
3 cups apricot nectar
1/4 cup agar agar flakes*

After soaking, simmer for 15 minutes, then stir in:

1/2 lb. tofu, blended   **1 1/2 cups carrots, shredded**
3 Tbsp. honey   **1/2 cup golden raisins**
2 cups walnuts or pecans, chopped   **1/2 tsp. vanilla**

After mixing all ingredients thoroughly together, pour into the mold or individual serving dishes. Chill until firm (about 4-6 hours or overnight). Remove from the mold and serve.

*See Molded Vegetable Salad on the opposite page.

Per Serving: Calories: 410, Protein: 10 gm., Fat: 23 gm., Carbohydrates: 10 gm.

Cucumber-Tomato Salad

Serves 6-8

Mix together in a salad bowl:

4 cups cucumbers, sliced   **1 cup celery, chopped**
3 cups tomatoes, chopped   **1/2 cup parsley, chopped**
2/3 cup onion, chopped

Dressing

Blend in a blender until smooth:

1/2 lb. tofu, mashed   **1/2 tsp. salt**
3 Tbsp. lime juice   **1/4 tsp. pepper**
1 tsp. sugar   **2 Tbsp. oil**

Mix dressing and vegetables and serve.

Per Serving: Calories: 128, Protein: 6 gm., Fat: 5 gm., Carbohydrates: 9 gm.

Frozen Fruit Salad

Serves 6
Makes 1 1/2 quarts

Blend in a blender until smooth and creamy:

1 lb. tofu   **1/4 cup lemon juice**
1/2 cup powdered sugar   **1 tsp. salt**
1/4 cup oil

Fold in:
4 cups drained fruit (fresh or canned)
1/2 cup pecans
2 tsp. crystallized ginger, chopped (optional)

Pour into individual serving dishes and freeze. Thaw for 15 minutes before serving.

Per Serving: Calories: 298, Protein: 7 gm., Fat: 19 gm., Carbohydrates: 4 gm.

Apple-Nut Salad

Mix together:
4 tart red apples
1/4 cup lemon juice
2 cups celery, diced
3/4 cup pecans, chopped

Pour boiling water to cover over:
1/2 cup raisins

Drain and add to the salad, then add:
1 1/2 cups Tofu Sour Creme Dressing, p. 41

Chill and serve.

Per Serving: Calories: 277, Protein: 5 gm., Fat: 20 gm., Carbohydrates: 23 gm.

Tofu Salad No. 1

This is good either as a sandwich spread or scooped on a piece of lettuce with tomato and garnished with parsley.

Mix together:

1 1/2 lbs. tofu, crumbled or mashed	**2 stalks celery, chopped fine**
1/2 cup Tofu Salad Dressing, p. 42	**1 1/2 tsp. garlic powder**
1/2 cup parsley, chopped	**1 1/2 tsp. salt**
1/4 cup pickle relish	**1/2 tsp. paprika**
1/2 medium onion, chopped fine	**1/4 tsp. black pepper**

Per Serving: Calories: 141, Protein: 12 gm., Fat: 6 gm., Carbohydrates: 11 gm.

Tofu Salad No. 2

Mash or crumble into a bowl:
1 lb. tofu

Mix in:

1/2 cup Tofu Salad Dressing, p. 42	**1 tsp. salt**
1/3 cup celery, chopped fine	**1/2 tsp. garlic powder**
1 Tbsp. fresh parsley, minced	**1/2 tsp. black pepper**
2 tsp. prepared mustard	**1/2 tsp. paprika**
1 tsp. onion powder	**1/4 tsp. tumeric**

Serve as a sandwich spread or on lettuce or tomato as a salad. Also good stuffed into a fresh bell pepper or ripe avocado as a salad.

Per Serving: Calories: 97, Protein: 7 gm., Fat: 7 gm., Carbohydrates: 4 gm.

Lettuce Rolls

Serves 6
Makes 24 rolls

Prepare Tofu Salad Dressing, p. 42.

Put in a mixing bowl:

1 lb. tofu, mashed
1/2 cup pitted black olives, sliced
1/4 cup sweet relish (optional)

3 green onions, chopped fine
2 stalks celery, chopped fine

Mix well and add:

1 1/2 cups Tofu Salad Dressing

Wash and dry the large outside leaves of a head of lettuce. Remove the stiff core piece from the leaves. Place 1/4 cup tofu mixture along one side of leaf and roll up. Cut each roll in 3″ sections and use toothpicks to keep roll snug.

Per Serving: Calories: 208, Protein: 10 gm., Fat: 16 gm., Carbohydrates: 9 gm.

Everybody's Tofu Salad

Serves 6
Makes 3 1/2 cups

From Everybody's Restaurant in Nashville, Tennessee.

Mix together:

1 lb. tofu, crumbled
1/3 cup onion, finely chopped
1/3 cup celery, finely chopped
3/4 cup Tofu Salad Dressing, p. 41
2 Tbsp. oil

1 1/2 tsp. salt
1/2 tsp. dill weed
2 Tbsp. toasted sesame seeds
4 tsp. pickle relish

Serve on lettuce as salad or in sandwiches.

Per Serving: Calories: 185, Protein: 9 gm., Fat: 14 gm., Carbohydrates: 6 gm.

Cottage Tofu Salad

Serves 6-8

Mix together:

1 lb. tofu, mashed or crumbled
1 Tbsp. fresh parsley

1 1/2 tsp. dried chives
1/4 tsp. dill weed

Blend in a blender until smooth and creamy:

1/2 cup tofu
1/4 cup oil
1 1/2 tsp. vinegar

1 1/2 tsp. lemon juice
1 tsp. salt
1/4-1/2 tsp. black pepper

Pour this into the mashed tofu mixture and mix well. Serve either as a sandwich spread or on lettuce or tomato as a salad.

Per Serving: Calories: 128, Protein: 6 gm., Fat: 11 gm., Carbohydrates: 2 gm.

Salad Dressings and Sauces

Clockwise from top left: Russian Dressing, Cucumber Salad Dressing, Thousand Island Dressing, Green Goddess Dressing, Dill Salad Dressing

SALAD DRESSINGS AND SAUCES

Salad dressings and sauces come out best with the very soft or "silken" type of tofu. Soft Japanese-style tofu will also work fine. You will get the smoothest dressing or sauce if you use a blender. Read "Blending Tofu" on p. 7. If you don't have a blender, you can use a food processor, electric mixer, or even a wire whip, resulting in varying degrees of smooth and creamy consistency. Use only very fresh tofu for salad dressings and sauces. If you are calorie-conscious, you can leave the oil out of any recipe and still have a creamy, tasty dressing.

Thousand Island Dressing

Makes 1 3/4 cups

Combine in a blender and blend until smooth and creamy:

1/2 lb. tofu, mashed
1/2 cup ketchup
2 Tbsp. oil

1/2 tsp. onion powder
1/8 tsp. garlic powder
1/4 tsp. salt

Fold in:

3 Tbsp. sweet pickle relish
3 Tbsp. stuffed green olives, minced
1 Tbsp. parsley, chopped fine

Per 1/4 Cup Serving: Calories: 89, Protein: 3 gm., Fat: 6 gm., Carbohydrates: 8 gm.

Dill Salad Dressing

Makes 1 1/4 cups

Combine in a blender:

1/2 lb. tofu, mashed
2 Tbsp. oil
1 Tbsp. vinegar

1/2 tsp. dill weed
1/2 tsp. salt
1/8 tsp. black pepper

Blend until smooth and creamy.

Per 1/4 Cup Serving: Calories: 79, Protein: 3 gm., Fat: 7 gm., Carbohydrates: 1 gm.

Cucumber Salad Dressing

Makes 1 3/4 cups

Combine in a blender:

1/2 lb. tofu, mashed
1 medium cucumber, peeled
2 Tbsp. oil

2 Tbsp. vinegar
1/2 tsp. salt
1/8 tsp. black pepper

Blend until smooth and creamy.

Per 1/4 Cup Serving: Calories: 63, Protein: 3 gm., Fat: 5 gm., Carbohydrates: 2 gm.

Green Goddess Dressing

Makes 1 3/4 cups

A San Francisco favorite with salad greens and avocado.

Combine in a blender:

1/2 lb. tofu, mashed   **1 tsp. onion powder**
1/4 cup oil   **1/8 tsp. black pepper**
1/2 Tbsp. dry chives   **1/4 tsp. garlic powder**
1/4 cup fresh parsley   **1/2 tsp. salt**
2 Tbsp. vinegar

Blend until smooth and creamy.

Per 1/4 Cup Serving: Calories: 93, Protein: 3 gm., Fat: 9 gm., Carbohydrates: 1 gm.

Creamy Italian Dressing

Makes 1 1/2 cups

Combine in a blender:

1/2 lb. tofu
1/2 cup oil
3 Tbsp. vinegar
1 tsp. salt
1/8 tsp. freshly ground black pepper

Blend until smooth and creamy.

Fold in:

4 cloves garlic, minced
2 Tbsp. sweet pickle relish with juice
1/4 tsp. oregano
1/8 tsp. red pepper flakes

Per 1/4 Cup Serving: Calories: 198, Protein: 3 gm., Fat: 20 gm., Carbohydrates: 4 gm.

Russian Dressing

Makes 1 1/2 cups

Combine in a blender:

1/2 lb. soft tofu   **1 Tbsp. prepared mustard**
1/3 cup ketchup   **1 tsp. onion powder**
2 Tbsp. vinegar   **1/2 tsp. salt**
2 Tbsp. oil

Blend until smooth and creamy.

Per 1/4 Cup Serving: Calories: 82, Protein: 3 gm., Fat: 6 gm., Carbohydrates: 7 gm.

Creamy Sweet-Sour Fruit Salad Dressing

Makes 2 1/2 cups

Combine in a blender:

1 cup oil	2 Tbsp. celery seed
1/2 cup tofu	1 1/2 tsp. dry mustard
1/2 cup sugar or honey	1 1/4 tsp. salt
1/2 cup vinegar	1 tsp. paprika
2 Tbsp. onion, minced	

Blend until smooth and creamy.

Per 1/4 Cup Serving: Calories: 240, Protein: 1 gm., Fat: 22 gm., Carbohydrates: 11 gm.

Sweet-Spicy Fruit Salad Dressing

Makes 1 3/4 cups

Combine in a blender:

1/2 lb. tofu, mashed	1/4 tsp. cinnamon
1/4 cup oil	1/4 tsp. vanilla
1/4 cup lemon juice	1/8 tsp. salt
1/4 cup honey	

Blend until smooth and creamy.

Per 1/4 Cup Serving: Calories: 131, Protein: 3 gm., Fat: 9 gm., Carbohydrates: 11 gm.

Tofu Sour Creme Dressing

Makes 1 1/4 cups

A versatile recipe you'll use again and again.

Combine in a blender:

1/2 lb. tofu	1 1/2 tsp. sugar
1/4 cup oil	1/2 tsp. salt
1 Tbsp. lemon juice	

Blend until smooth and creamy.

Per 1/4 Cup Serving: Calories: 134, Protein: 4 gm., Fat: 13 gm., Carbohydrates: 3 gm.

Creamy Sweet-Sour Fruit Salad Dressing

Avocado Salad Dressing

Makes 1 1/4 cups

Combine in a blender:
  1 ripe avocado (about 3/4 cup)
  1/2 cup Tofu Salad Dressing, p. 42
  1 Tbsp. fresh lemon juice
  1/2 tsp. salt
  1/4 tsp. garlic powder
  1/8 tsp. black pepper

Blend until smooth and creamy.

Per 1/4 Cup Serving: Calories: 107, Protein: 2 gm., Fat: 10 gm., Carbohydrates: 3 gm.

Tofu Salad Dressing

Makes 1 1/2 cups

A basic creamy dressing for salads and sandwiches.

Combine in a blender:
  1/2 lb. soft tofu   **1 1/2 tsp. prepared mustard**
  1/4 cup oil   **1 tsp. vinegar**
  1 Tbsp. lemon juice   **1/2 tsp. salt**
  1 Tbsp. sugar

Blend until smooth and creamy.

Per 1/4 Cup Serving: Calories: 116, Protein: 3 gm., Fat: 11 gm., Carbohydrates: 3 gm.

Tartare Sauce

Makes 2 1/2 cups

Combine in a blender and blend until smooth and creamy:
  1/2 lb. tofu, mashed   **1 tsp. prepared mustard**
  1/4 cup vinegar   **3/4 tsp. salt**
  2 Tbsp. oil   **1/2 cup onion, chopped**
  2 Tbsp. sugar

Fold in:
  1/4 cup sweet pickle relish

Per 1/4 Cup Serving: Calories: 61, Protein: 2 gm., Fat: 4 gm., Carbohydrates: 6 gm.

Hollandaise Sauce No. 1

Makes 1 3/4 cups

Combine in a blender:

1/2 lb. tofu
1/2 tsp. salt
1/2 cup oil
1/2 tsp. sugar

1/4 cup fresh lemon juice
1/8 tsp. black pepper
a few grains cayenne

Blend until smooth and creamy. This can be heated and served hot, but be careful not to let it boil.

Per 1/4 Cup Serving: Calories: 165, Protein: 3 gm., Fat: 17 gm., Carbohydrates: 2 gm.

Hollandaise Sauce No. 2

Makes 2 cups

Combine in a blender:

1/2 lb. tofu
1/2 cup oil
7 Tbsp. lemon juice

1/2 tsp. salt
1/8 tsp. black pepper

Blend until smooth and creamy. This can be heated and served hot, but be careful not to let it boil.

Per 1/4 Cup Serving: Calories: 192, Protein: 3 gm., Fat: 20 gm., Carbohydrates: 2 gm.

Horseradish Sauce

Makes 1 cup

Combine in a blender:

1/2 cup tofu, mashed
3 Tbsp. prepared horseradish
1 1/2 Tbsp. oil

1 1/2 Tbsp. vinegar
1 tsp. sugar
1/2 tsp. salt

Blend until smooth and creamy.

Per 1/4 Cup Serving: Calories: 77, Protein: 2 gm., Fat: 7 gm., Carbohydrates: 2 gm.

Main Dishes

Barbecued Tofu and Picnic Potato Salad

MAIN DISHES

Spaghetti Primavera

Serves 4-6

This recipe is pictured on p. 4.

Cut into 2″ x 1/2″ x 1/8″ pieces:
1 lb. firm tofu

Marinate the pieces for 2 hours in a mixture of:
1/4 cup soy sauce
2 Tbsp. wine vinegar
2 Tbsp. oil

Brown the marinated tofu pieces lightly in:
2 Tbsp. oil
the leftover marinade

Set aside.

Boil until almost tender in 1″ boiling water:
4 cups broccoli flowerettes (fresh or frozen)
1 1/2 cups peas (fresh or frozen)

Drain and reserve water.

Saute together:
1 Tbsp. oil
1 cup fresh mushrooms, sliced

Sauce

Let bubble together over low heat for 3 minutes:
1/3 cup oil
1/3 cup unbleached white flour

Whisk in without making lumps:
3 cups liquid (reserved cooking water, milk or soymilk)

Add:
1/2 cup fresh parsley, chopped   **1/2 tsp. garlic powder**
1 1/2 tsp. salt   **1/8 tsp. cayenne**

Continue cooking over low heat and stirring until thickened and smooth. Add tofu, vegetables and mushrooms to the sauce and serve hot over spaghetti noodles.

Variation: Substitute 2 cups broccoli flowerettes and 2 cups asparagus spears for the 4 cups broccoli flowerettes.

Per Serving: Calories: 481, Protein: 12 gm., Fat: 14 gm., Carbohydrates: 15 gm.

Curried Tofu and Nuts Over Noodles   *Serves 4-6*

Freeze, thaw, squeeze out and cut in 3/4" cubes:
1 1/2 lbs. tofu

Marinate the tofu cubes for 1 hour in a mixture of:

1 1/2 Tbsp. peanut butter   **1 Tbsp. honey**
1/4 cup oil   **1 Tbsp. curry powder**
3 Tbsp. soy sauce   **1/2 tsp. black pepper**
1 tsp. onion powder

Preheat oven to 375° F.

Spread a cookie sheet with 1 tablespoon oil, then put on the marinated cubes and bake for 10 minutes. Turn the cubes over and bake 5 more minutes.

Fry over high heat for about 3 minutes:
1 Tbsp. oil
8 scallions, cut in 1 1/2" pieces

Set aside. In a saucepan whisk together over low heat and cook until thickened:
1 cup water
2 Tbsp. soy sauce
1 Tbsp. cornstarch

Add the baked tofu cubes and scallions to the sauce along with:
1 cup roasted blanched almonds (or other nuts)

Stir all together and serve hot over noodles.

Per Serving: Calories: 486, Protein: 18 gm., Fat: 41 gm., Carbohydrates: 19 gm.

Sesame Tofu   *Serves 6*

Cut into 3/4" cubes or 1/4" thick slices:
2 lbs. firm tofu

Marinate for 2 hours in a mixture of:

1/3 cup soy sauce   **1 Tbsp. ginger root, grated or**
1/4 cup oil   **1/4 tsp. ginger**
2 cloves garlic, minced or   **2 tsp. sugar**
1/4 tsp. garlic powder

Roll in:
1/2 cup sesame seeds

Brown in oil. Serve hot with rice.

Per Serving: Calories: 206, Protein: 13 gm., Fat: 15 gm., Carbohydrates: 7 gm.

Tofu Rancheros

Serves 4-6

This is an adaptation of a classic Mexican dish that is traditionally served for breakfast with refried pinto beans and sweet coffee. The "ranchero" sauce derives its name from being made rapidly in one frying pan, as if over an open fire "en un rancho."

Prepare vegetables and set aside:
6 large or 8 medium tomatoes, wedged   **3 cloves garlic, chopped**
3 medium onions, wedged   **1/4 cup fresh parsley or cilantro, chopped**

Slice into 12 slices and sprinkle with salt:
2 lbs. tofu

In a heavy skillet, heat over medium heat:
1/4 cup oil

Fry for 2 seconds on each side:
8 to 12 corn tortillas

Tortillas should be heated but soft. Put 2 tortillas on each plate, side by side.

In the same pan, quickly brown the tofu slices on each side, adding more oil if necessary. Place 2-3 slices on each plate. Immediately add onion wedges and chopped garlic to the hot pan. When browned add tomato wedges. Cover and steam for 2-3 minutes, stirring occasionally.

Remove lid and stir in:
1 (6 oz.) can chopped green chilies   **salt and black pepper to taste**
1 pinch ground or crushed cumin

When tomatoes are soft and saucy but before they lose their shape completely, remove from heat and pour equally over the plates with tortillas and tofu. Serve immediately, garnished with the chopped parsley or cilantro.

Per Serving: Calories: 501, Protein: 23 gm., Fat: 30 gm., Carbohydrates: 41 gm.

Apricot-Orange Barbecue

Serves 4-6

Preheat oven to 350° F.

Slice into 1/4" slices and lightly fry:
1 lb. firm tofu

Arrange the fried slices in a baking dish. Saute together until transparent:
1 Tbsp. oil
1/4 cup onions, chopped

Stir in:
6 Tbsp. apricot jam   **1/2 tsp. coriander**
5 Tbsp. frozen orange juice concentrate   **1/2 tsp. salt**
5 Tbsp. water   **1/2 tsp. ginger**
2 Tbsp. prepared mustard   **1/8 tsp. garlic powder**
1 Tbsp. vinegar   **1/16-1/8 tsp. cayenne (optional)**

Pour the sauce over the tofu and bake 10-15 minutes, until bubbling.

Per Serving: Calories: 212, Protein: 8 gm., Fat: 6 gm., Carbohydrates: 20 gm.

Seaside Cakes

Let bubble together over low heat for 1-2 minutes:
1/4 cup oil
1/4 cup unbleached white flour

Whip in slowly, leaving no lumps:
1 cup milk or soymilk
1/2 tsp. salt

Stir in and continue cooking until very thick:
2 Tbsp. onion, minced

Combine in a bowl:
1 lb. tofu, crumbled   **1/2 tsp. dry mustard**
1 tsp. salt   **dash of cayenne**

Mix the white sauce into the tofu mix. Chill 3-4 hours. Shape the chilled mixture into cakes 2 1/2" round by 1/2" thick.

Then roll cakes in a mixture of:
12-16 soda crackers, crushed to crumbs
1 1/2 tsp. paprika

Chill the crumb-covered cakes about 1 hour. (At this point the cakes can be frozen for later use.)

Fry the cakes in:
2-3 Tbsp. oil per pan

Turn them gently, browning on both sides. Serve with lemon wedges, tartare sauce, or cocktail sauce and garnish with parsley or watercress.

Per Serving: Calories: 313, Protein: 8 gm., Fat: 27 gm., Carbohydrates: 11 gm.

Tofu Spinach Pie

Preheat oven to 400° F.

Have ready:
1 (10 oz.) pkg. frozen chopped spinach, steamed
1 partially baked 9" pie shell

Saute together until soft:
1/3 cup oil
1 1/2 cups onions, chopped

Add and saute for 2 minutes more:
the steamed spinach

Mix this together with:
1 1/2 lbs. tofu, crumbled   **1 Tbsp. lemon juice**
1 tsp. garlic powder   **1 1/2 tsp. salt**

Pour into a partially-baked pie shell. Bake for about 30 minutes, until crust is golden.

Per Serving: Calories: 433, Protein: 15 gm., Fat: 32 gm., Carbohydrates: 8 gm.

Chili Con Tofu With Beans

This is Southwestern-Style Chili made with frozen tofu and chili broth.

Have ready:
5 cups cooked pinto beans

Reserve the cooking water or liquid in the cans with the beans.

Freeze, thaw, squeeze out and tear into bite-size pieces:
2 lbs. tofu

Whip together in a mixing bowl:
1/4 cup soy sauce
1 1/2 Tbsp. tomato paste
2 Tbsp. peanut butter
1/2 Tbsp. onion powder
1/4 tsp. garlic powder
1/2 cup water
2 Tbsp. oil

Add to this the frozen tofu pieces and mix until all are evenly coated. Then fry the seasoned tofu in 1/4 cup oil over medium heat until all liquid is absorbed and tofu is well browned.

In another pan, saute until onions are transparent:
2 Tbsp. oil
1 large green pepper, diced
2 large onions, diced
3 cloves garlic, minced

Add these and the browned tofu to the cooked beans in a cooking pot, with reserved cooking water to cover all (water can be added if needed).

Add also to the pot:
1 Tbsp. salt
3 Tbsp. chili powder
1 1/2 Tbsp. cumin

Bring to a simmer and serve hot with Sesame Tofu Crackers, p. 121, and salad.

Per Serving: Calories: 377, Protein: 20 gm., Fat: 19 gm., Carbohydrates: 19 gm.

Chili Con Tofu

Serves 6

This is American-Style Chili with tomato broth.

Have ready:
**2 1/2 cups cooked pinto beans and
1 cup bean broth or water**

Stir together in a bowl:
1 lb. tofu, crumbled   **1 1/2 tsp. salt**
1/2 tsp. garlic powder   **3 Tbsp. Worcestershire sauce (optional)**
1/2 tsp. chili powder

Mix together well.

Saute together until the tofu is browned:
**2 Tbsp. oil
1 small onion, diced
1 clove garlic, minced
the tofu mixture**

Bring to a boil in a saucepan:
2 cups tomato sauce   **pinch black pepper**
1 cup bean broth   **1 1/2 Tbsp. chili powder**
1 cup water   **1 tsp. cumin**
2 tsp. salt

Add the cooked pinto beans and the browned tofu. When throughly heated, serve with crackers.

Per Serving: Calories: 332, Protein: 18 gm., Fat: 8 gm., Carbohydrates: 28 gm.

Tofu Burgers

Serves 6
Makes twelve 3" burgers

Combine in a bowl:
2 lbs. tofu, mashed   **1/4 tsp. black pepper**
2 cups whole grain bread crumbs, fine **1 tsp. salt**
1 Tbsp. soy sauce   **1/2 cup celery, chopped fine**
1 tsp. garlic powder   **2 tsp. onion powder**

Mix well. Form into 3" patties.

Roll in breading mixture of:
**1/2 cup cornmeal
1/4 cup unbleached white flour
1/4 tsp. salt**

Fry in skillet with 1/4" oil. Brown on both sides. Drain on paper, serve hot on a bun with garnishes or plain.

Per Serving: Calories: 364, Protein: 18 gm., Fat: 16 gm., Carbohydrates: 40 gm.

Stir-Fry Chinese Cabbage and Tofu   *Serves 6*

Have ready:
 1 lb. tofu, cut in 1″ x 1/2″ x 1/4″ pieces
 1/2 tsp. ginger root, peeled and finely diced
 1/4 tsp. vegetarian bouillon, dissolved in 2 Tbsp. water
 1 1/2 tsp. cornstarch, mixed into 2 Tbsp. water
 4 cups Chinese cabbage, chopped and separated into crunchy and leafy parts
 2 cloves garlic, crushed

Cut the crunchy parts of the Chinese cabbage into 1″ wide pieces. Cut leafy parts into small pieces.

Heat in a wok or heavy skillet:
 2 Tbsp. oil

Add chopped ginger and one clove crushed garlic. Let them fry until brown, then remove. Add the sliced tofu and stir to cover all with the flavored oil.

Add:
 1 Tbsp. soy sauce
 1/4 tsp. salt

Stir and cook for 2 minutes. Remove from pan with all juices.

In the same pan, heat:
 1 Tbsp. oil

Add the other crushed garlic, fry until brown. Remove. Add the crunchy sections of the Chinese cabbage and stir. Cook for 1 minute.

Add:
 the dissolved bouillon
 1/4 tsp. salt

Cover and steam 2 minutes. Add the leafy sections of the cabbage and stir. Cover and cook for 1 minute. Return the tofu to the pan. Dribble the cornstarch mixture into the center of the pan where the juices are, stir and cook until thickened and serve immediately.

Per Serving: Calories: 148, Protein: 7 gm., Fat: 12 gm., Carbohydrates: 4 gm.

Walnut Broccoli Stir-Fry

Serves 4-5

Cut and brown lightly:
1 lb. firm tofu, cut into 1" cubes
2 Tbsp. oil

Bring to a boil:
1 cup water
1/2 tsp. salt

Drop into boiling salted water, boil one minute, drain and reserve the liquid:
2 carrots, sliced thin
2 cups broccoli flowerettes, with 1" or 2" stems

In a wok or large frying pan, saute over medium heat until soft:
2 Tbsp. oil
2 onions, thinly sliced

Then add:
1 cup mushrooms, sliced
1 cup walnut halves

Increase heat to medium high and add the carrots and broccoli. Stir. Add tofu cubes, stir again.

To the reserved vegetable stock, add:
1 Tbsp. cornstarch   **1/2 tsp. freshly ground black pepper**
3 Tbsp. soy sauce

Pour over the vegetables and tofu, then stir and cook everything until bubbling. Serve hot over rice or Chinese noodles.

Per Serving: Calories: 407, Protein: 18 gm., Fat: 31 gm., Carbohydrates: 13 gm.

Potato-Tofu Casserole

Serves 6

Preheat oven to 325° F.

Mix together in a bowl:
3 cups potatoes, mashed   **1/4 tsp. black pepper**
1 1/2 lbs. tofu, mashed   **1/4 tsp. garlic powder**
1 1/4 tsp. salt   **1/4 cup fresh parsley, chopped**

Saute together:
2 Tbsp. oil
1 medium onion, chopped

When onions are limp, mix into the potato-tofu mixture. Spread into an oiled 8" x 8" x 2" baking dish, and sprinkle with paprika. Bake for 35 minutes.

Per Serving: Calories: 253, Protein: 11 gm., Fat: 17 gm., Carbohydrates: 4 gm.

Walnut Broccoli Stir-Fry

Filet de Tofu

Serves 6-8

Tofu that smells slightly sour can be used in this recipe.

Cut into 1/2" to 5/8" slices:
2 lbs. tofu

Boil the slices in salted water for 20 minutes, adding a bit of seaweed to water if you like. Drain and let cool.

Preheat oven to 350° F.

Lay the slices out close together in a shallow pan and sprinkle with:
1 tsp. paprika   **1 tsp. salt**
2 Tbsp. parsley, minced   **1/2 tsp. black pepper**
1 tsp. chives, chopped fine

Carefully pour in and around the tofu pieces, not disturbing the herbs, until it reaches the top of the slices:
vegetable bouillon (about 12 oz.)

Bake for about 20 minutes or until almost all liquid is gone. Remove pan from the oven and pour more of the liquid on in the same manner as before. Bake another 10 minutes until liquid is almost gone again.

Brush with:
olive oil

Squeeze on:
fresh lemon juice to taste

Then broil until lightly browned. Serve garnished with parsley and lemon wedges.

Per Serving: Calories: 110, Protein: 10 gm., Fat: 7 gm., Carbohydrates: 3 gm.

Indonesian Sate

Serves 4
Makes one 9" x 13" pan

Mash:
2 cloves garlic

Add and beat in:
1/2 tsp. vinegar   **2 tsp. honey**
1/4 cup peanut butter   **1/4 cup soy sauce**
2 Tbsp. oil   **1/4 cup boiling water**
1 tsp. fresh ginger root, grated   **1/2 tsp. salt**
1/4 tsp. bay leaf, ground   **1/8 tsp. cayenne (more if you like)**

Slice into 1/2" slices:
1 lb. tofu

Oil the bottom of a 9" x 13" baking dish, then cover the bottom with a thin layer of the sauce. Place the slices of tofu in the dish, one layer thick, then pour on the rest of the sauce. Let sit and marinate for 2-3 hours. Bake at 375° F. for 20-25 minutes. Serve with rice and vegetables.

Per Serving: Calories: 345, Protein: 14 gm., Fat: 29 gm., Carbohydrates: 11 gm.

Barbecued Tofu

Using frozen tofu lends a chewy texture. This recipe is pictured on p. 44.

Freeze, thaw, squeeze out and cut in 1" x 3" strips:
2 lbs. firm tofu

Mix together:

3 Tbsp. peanut butter	**1/4 tsp. black pepper**
1/3 cup oil	**1/2 tsp. garlic powder**
1 Tbsp. paprika	**2 tsp. salt**

Whip until smooth. Pour over tofu strips and squeeze in as evenly as possible. Marinate 1 hour. While it is marinating, prepare Barbecue Sauce, below.

Preheat oven to 350° F.

Lay tofu out on cookie sheet which has been spread with 1/4 cup oil. Bake at 350° F. for 25 minutes or until bottoms are browned. Then turn the pieces over and bake about 25 more minutes, or until other sides are browned. Pour Barbecue Sauce over all the pieces and bake 15 more minutes. Serve.

Barbecue Sauce

Saute together until onions are transparent:
1/3 cup oil
1 medium onion, chopped
2 cloves of garlic, minced

Stir in:

2 1/2 cups tomato sauce	**1 tsp. allspice**
1/4 cup water	**1 Tbsp. crushed red pepper or**
1 cup brown sugar	**3/4 tsp. cayenne powder**
1 Tbsp. molasses	**1 1/2 tsp. dried parsley**
1/2 cup salad mustard	**or 1 Tbsp. fresh parsley**
1 1/2 tsp. salt	

Bring to a boil, reduce heat and simmer for about one hour.

Add and simmer 10-15 minutes more:
1/2 cup lemon juice
2 Tbsp. soy sauce

Per Serving: Calories: 664, Protein: 16 gm., Fat: 44 gm., Carbohydrates: 71 gm.

Lasagne

Serves 6-8
Makes one 9" x 13" pan

Have ready:
Basic Italian-Style Tomato Sauce, p. 65,
or 7 cups ready-made tomato sauce
Ricotta-Style Filling, opposite page

Cook and drain:
1/2 lb. lasagne noodles

Preheat oven to 350° F.

Start making layers in a 9" x 13" pan, starting with a thin layer of tomato sauce, then a layer of cooked noodles, then a layer of half of the Ricotta-Style Filling. Continue in the same order, using half the remaining tomato sauce, noodles, the remaining tofu, and ending with the remaining tomato sauce. Bake for about 30 minutes.

Per Serving: Calories: 465, Protein: 23 gm., Fat: 21 gm., Carbohydrates: 53 gm.

Mushroom Tofu Over Noodles

Serves 4-6

Freeze, thaw, squeeze out and cut into 3" x 1 1/2" x 1/2" pieces:
1 1/2 lbs. tofu

Marinate the tofu pieces for 2 hours in a mixture of:
3 Tbsp. peanut butter   **1 tsp. Kitchen Bouquet**
1/4 cup oil   **1/4 tsp. garlic powder**
3 Tbsp. soy sauce

Preheat oven to 375° F.

Spread a cookie sheet with 1 tablespoon oil, then lay the marinated tofu pieces on the sheet. Bake for 10 minutes. Turn the pieces over and bake 10 minutes more.

Prepare Dark Mushroom Gravy, below.

Dark Mushroom Gravy

Saute together:
2 Tbsp. oil
1/2 lb. fresh mushrooms, sliced

Whisk together over low heat until thick:
1 1/2 cups water
1 Tbsp. cornstarch
1/2 tsp. Kitchen Bouquet

Add sauteed mushrooms. Arrange the baked tofu pieces on a platter of noodles, then pour the gravy over all. Serve hot.

Per Serving: Calories: 333, Protein: 14 gm., Fat: 29 gm., Carbohydrates: 8 gm.

Eggplant Lasagne

Have ready:
**3 cups Italian-Style Tomato Sauce, p. 65,
or ready-made Italian Sauce**

Ricotta-Style Filling

Grind through a food mill:
3 lbs. firm tofu

Mix in:

1/2 cup fresh lemon juice	**6 Tbsp. oil**
4 tsp. sugar or honey	**4 tsp. basil**
2 tsp. salt	**1 tsp. garlic powder**

Wash, peel and cut into 1/4" slices:
2 medium eggplants

Soak the slices in cold salted water for 5 minutes.

Preheat oven to 350° F.

Drain and then dredge the eggplant slices in a mixture of:
1 1/4 cups unbleached white flour
1/2 cup cornmeal
1 tsp. oregano flakes
2 medium cloves garlic, crushed
1/2 tsp. salt
dash of freshly ground black pepper

Lay the slices on an oiled cookie sheet and oven-fry for 8-10 minutes or until golden brown. Turn the slices over, spread 2 tablespoons more oil on the pan and brown the other sides.

Cover the bottom of a 9" x 13" pan with:
1 cup Italian-Style Tomato Sauce

Then make a layer of the oven-fried eggplant and on top of that spread a thick layer of the tofu mixture, saving 1/2 cup for the top. Next make another layer of the oven-fried eggplant.

Pour on:
2 cups Italian-Style Tomato Sauce

Sprinkle the remaining 1/2 cup tofu mixture over the top. Bake at 350° F. for about 35 minutes, until slightly browned on top. Serve with a tossed green salad and garlic bread.

Per Serving: Calories: 520, Protein: 22 gm., Fat: 29 gm., Carbohydrates: 48 gm.

Kalatsoonya

This is a traditional Cretan recipe made in the spring when the first onion greens appear.

Combine in a large bowl:

2 lbs. tofu, crumbled
2 cups fresh spinach, coarsely chopped
juice from 3 small lemons
1/4 cup fresh green onion tops,
  chopped fine
1 Tbsp. salt

5 tsp. fresh mint, chopped fine
  or 3/4 tsp. dried mint
2 tsp. fresh basil, chopped fine
  or 3/4 tsp. dried basil
1/4 tsp. garlic powder
1/8 tsp. black pepper

Set aside.

Combine in a medium bowl:

3 cups unbleached white flour
1 cup water
3/4 tsp. salt

Mix and knead the dough on a board floured with 2 tablespoons unbleached white flour until it forms a smooth ball. Divide into 2 parts and roll out thin on the floured board, about 1/8" thick, with a rolling pin. Make sure the dough and the board are floured to keep from sticking.

The Cretan women do this with a long smooth stick from the *mourna* or mulberry tree. You can use a clean, sanded broomstick if you want to try it. First roll and pat the dough somewhat flat with your hands and give it a few rolls with your broomstick.

Then dust your workspace and the dough with flour. Starting at the edge nearest you, flip the edge over the stick and slowly roll the whole piece up, smoothing the rolled dough outward with a circular motion of your palms. Do not press down. When you get it all rolled up, unroll it, dust with flour again, turn the dough over and start again. The Cretan women can roll their dough out to table-top size in just a few minutes.

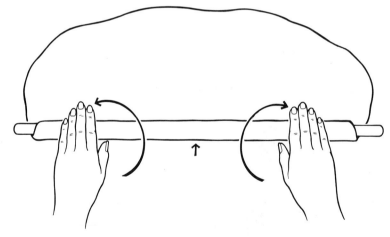

Cut the rolled dough (called filo, FEE-lo) into 4" x 4" squares. You can patch the edge pieces together to make squares. Put 3 tablespoons of filling in the center of each square and fold the 4 corners into the center. Pinch and pat slightly to seal so the filling will not leak out.

In a heavy skillet put:

1/4" olive oil

Set over medium heat. It will be ready when you can smell the fragrance of the olive oil (do not let it smoke). Carefully put in the Kalatsoonya, one by one, folded side up. Fry on both sides until golden brown. Drain on absorbent paper. These are good hot and even better the next day.

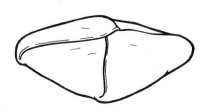

Per Serving: Calories: 248, Protein: 15 gm., Fat: 18 gm., Carbohydrates: 8 gm.

Tofu Loaf

Serves 6-8
Makes one loaf pan

Preheat oven to 350° F.

Mix together:
  1 1/2 lbs. tofu, mashed
  1/3 cup ketchup
  1/3 cup soy sauce
  2 Tbsp. dijon mustard
  1/2 cup parsley, chopped
  1/4 tsp. black pepper
  1 medium onion, chopped fine
  1/4 tsp. garlic powder
  1 cup whole grain bread crumbs, rolled oats,
   or corn flakes, crushed

Mix all ingredients together. Put 1/4 cup oil in a loaf pan, then press the mixture into the pan. Bake for about 1 hour. Let cool 10-15 minutes before trying to remove from pan. Garnish with ketchup and parsley. Also good sliced and fried for sandwiches the next day.

Per Serving: Calories: 226, Protein: 10 gm., Fat: 13 gm., Carbohydrates: 18 gm.

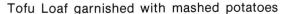

Tofu Loaf garnished with mashed potatoes

Tofu Foo Yung

Serves 6

In a skillet or wok, saute over low heat for about 5 minutes:
- **2 Tbsp. oil**
- **1 cup snow peas, cut in 1" pieces**
- **1 cup fresh mushrooms, sliced**
- **8 green onions, cut in 1 1/2" pieces**
- **1 (8 oz.) can water chestnuts, sliced**

When vegetables are crisp-tender, mix in:
- **2 cups fresh bean sprouts**

Remove from heat and set aside.

Preheat oven to 325° F.

Blend until smooth and creamy:
- **1 3/4 lbs. tofu**
- **2 Tbsp. soy sauce**

Pour this into a bowl and mix in:
- **1/2 cup tofu, mashed**
- **3/4 cup unbleached white flour**
- **3 Tbsp. nutritional yeast (optional)**
- **2 tsp. baking powder**

Mix vegetables and tofu mixture together well. On an oiled cookie sheet, make six to eight 5" rounds about 1/2" thick, using about 1/2 cup of the mixture for each round. Leave about 1" space between the rounds. Bake for 30 minutes, flip over and bake 15 minutes more. Serve hot over rice or noodles with Mushroom Gravy, below.

Mushroom Gravy

Mix together in a saucepan:
- **2 cups cold water**
- **4 Tbsp. soy sauce**
- **2 Tbsp. cornstarch**
- **1/2 cup fresh mushrooms, diced small**

Cook over low heat, stirring until thickened.

Per Serving: Calories: 262, Protein: 17 gm., Fat: 13 gm., Carbohydrates: 22 gm.

Tofu Spaghetti Balls

Serves 4-6
Makes twenty-four 1 1/2" balls

Mix together well:
3/4 lb. tofu, mashed
1/2 cup flour, bread crumbs,
 rolled oats, or corn flakes
1 1/2 Tbsp. peanut butter
3 Tbsp. soy sauce
1/4 cup fresh parsley, chopped fine
1 small onion, chopped fine
1/2 tsp. dry mustard
1/8 tsp. black pepper

Roll into 1 1/2" balls. Roll balls in flour and fry in 1/2" oil over medium heat until browned all over. Turn each ball about every 3 minutes. Serve with hot spaghetti and Basic Italian-Style Tomato Sauce, opposite page.

Per Ball: *Calories: 58, Protein: 2 gm.,*
            Fat: 4 gm., Carbohydrates: 3 gm.

Tofu Spaghetti Balls

Basic Italian-Style Tomato Sauce

Serves 4-6
Makes 7 cups

Saute until tender:
1/2 cup olive oil
1 medium onion, diced
2 carrots, diced
2 celery stalks, diced

Add:
6 cups tomato sauce
1 Tbsp. dried basil
1/2 cup fresh parsley, chopped
3 cloves garlic, minced
2 Tbsp. wine vinegar
1 tsp. salt

Simmer over low heat for 30 minutes. This sauce can be blended (after being cooled) for a smooth sauce.

Per 1 Cup Serving: Calories: 231, Protein: 4 gm., Fat: 16 gm., Carbohydrates: 21 gm.

Greco-Italian Pasta With Tofu

Serves 6

Put on water sufficient to boil:
1 lb. macaroni

Cut in 1/4" cubes:
1 1/2 lbs. firm tofu

Fry tofu cubes until crispy brown in:
3 Tbsp. oil

In another pan, simmer together for a couple of minutes:
1/4 cup oil
2 Tbsp. basil
2 Tbsp. oregano
2 Tbsp. parsley
1 tsp. salt

Blend together in a blender:
1 cup water
2 Tbsp. unbleached white flour

Stir this mixture slowly into the simmering herbs and continue stirring until thickened.

Stir in:
1 Tbsp. garlic granules
1 cup raisins

Mix the tofu with the sauce along with:
1 1/2 cup walnuts, coarsely chopped

Immediately toss into the macaroni and serve.

Per Serving: Calories: 546, Protein: 16 gm., Fat: 37 gm., Carbohydrates: 44 gm.

Enchiladas

(This recipe is pictured on the cover.)

Enchiladas are traditionally served with refried pinto beans, Spanish Rice and tossed salad.

Freeze, thaw, squeeze and tear into bite-size pieces:
   3 lbs. tofu

Have ready:
   16-20 masa (corn) tortillas or Flour Tortillas, p. 117

Whip together:
   1/4 cup soy sauce
   2 Tbsp. tomato paste
   2 Tbsp. peanut butter
   2 tsp. onion powder
   1 tsp. cumin powder

Mix this together well with the tofu pieces and brown in 1/2 cup oil, turning often. While tofu is browning, prepare either Chili Gravy or Tomato Sauce, below.

Chili Gravy

Fry until soft:
   6 Tbsp. oil
   1 large onion, chopped fine

Mix together in a separate bowl:
   6 Tbsp. chili powder
   6 Tbsp. white flour
   1 tsp. cumin
   1 1/4 tsp. salt
   1 tsp. garlic powder

Add this to the soft onions, then whip in slowly without making lumps:
   1 1/2 qts. water

Bring to a boil and boil 20 minutes.

Tomato Sauce

Saute together:
   2 Tbsp. oil
   1 cup onion, diced
   7 cloves garlic, pressed

When onions are transparent, add:

3 (15 oz.) cans tomato sauce	**1 Tbsp. cumin powder**
3 1/2 cups water	**2 tsp. salt**
1/2 cup chili powder	

Simmer for 1/2 hour.

(Enchiladas, continued on next page)

(Enchiladas, continued)

Preheat oven to 350° F.

With tongs, submerge each corn tortilla in hot oil (350° F.) for just 1 or 2 seconds, to soften. (If you are using Flour Tortillas, skip this step and dunk directly in the Chili Gravy or Tomato Sauce.) Wipe off excess oil on edge of pan and dip the tortilla into the Chili Gravy or Tomato Sauce, then lay it on a plate. Lay 1/3-1/2 cup of browned tofu across the tortilla and roll it up. Pour a thin layer of Chili Gravy or Tomato Sauce in the bottom of a 9" x 13" baking pan and arrange the rolled tortillas in it. Cover with the rest of the Chili Gravy or Tomato Sauce and bake for about 20-25 minutes or until bubbling.

Variation: Before baking sprinkle over the top:
1 1/2 cups onions, chopped
1 1/2 cups black olives, chopped

Per Serving (With Chili Gravy): Calories: 669, Protein: 24 gm., Fat: 50 gm., Carbohydrates: 37 gm.

Per Serving (With Tomato Sauce): Calories: 654, Protein: 27 gm., Fat: 42 gm., Carbohydrates: 50 gm.

Peasant Pie

Makes one 9" deep-dish pie

Have ready:
1 unbaked 9" deep-dish pie shell
6 medium potatoes, boiled (about 4 cups)

Freeze, thaw, squeeze out and cut into bite-size pieces:
1 lb. tofu

Marinate the tofu for 1 hour in a mixture of:
1/4 cup soy sauce
2 Tbsp. oil
1/2 tsp. garlic powder

Saute together:
3 Tbsp. oil　　　　　　　　　　　**1/2 lbs. mushrooms, sliced**
2 cups onions, chopped in 1/2" pieces　**2 cloves garlic, pressed**
1 cup celery, chopped in 1/4" pieces

Set aside when tender. Lightly brown the tofu and its marinade in another pan, then mix it together with the vegetables and put them in the unbaked pie shell.

Preheat oven to 375° F.

Mash the boiled potatoes with enough of the cooking water to be fluffy.

Whip in:
1/4 cup oil
1 tsp. salt

Spread the whipped potatoes over the top of the pie. Bake for about 45 minutes.

Per Serving: Calories: 492, Protein: 13 gm., Fat: 32 gm., Carbohydrates: 26 gm.

Tamale Pie

Freeze, thaw, squeeze out and cut into bite-size pieces:
1 1/2 lbs. tofu

Mix together:
3 Tbsp. soy sauce
2 Tbsp. peanut butter
2 tsp. onion powder
1/4 tsp. garlic

Work this mixture into the tofu pieces and mix until all the pieces are coated.

Brown the tofu pieces in:
2-3 Tbsp. oil

Saute in another pan until soft:
2 Tbsp. oil
1 large onion, chopped
1 large bell pepper, chopped
1 clove garlic, minced

Add:
1 (28 oz.) can whole tomatoes
1 (15 oz.) can tomato sauce
1/4 cup chili powder
1/2 tsp. oregano
1 tsp. cumin
1 tsp. salt
1 (15 oz). can whole pitted black olives, drained
the browned tofu
1 (1 lb.) pkg. frozen cut corn
2 (6 oz.) cans green chilies

Mix well and pour into a 3-quart casserole.

Preheat oven to 350° F.

Cover with Cornbread Topping, below, before baking.

Cornbread Topping

Mix together in a bowl:
1 1/2 cups cornmeal   **1 tsp. salt**
1 1/2 cups unbleached white flour   **2 Tbsp. sugar**
3 1/2 tsp. baking powder

Stir in:
1 1/2 cups water, milk or soymilk
1/3 cup oil

Bake for about 45 minutes or until cornbread is done.

Per Serving: Calories: 657, Protein: 20 gm., Fat: 30 gm., Carbohydrates: 85 gm.

Tofu Pot Pie

Have ready:
**bottom and top crusts for a
9 1/2" deep dish pie**

Bake the bottom crust at 400° F. for 10 minutes.

Filling

Cut into 3/4" cubes:
1 1/2 lbs. firm tofu

Mix together and then mix with the cubes:
**1/4 cup unbleached white flour
2 tsp. salt
1/2 tsp. black pepper
1/2 tsp. garlic powder**

Brown the coated cubes over medium-high heat in:
1/4 cup oil

When the cubes are brown and crispy, add:
**1 cup carrots, sliced thin
1 cup celery, sliced thin
1 1/2 cups onion, chopped
1 cup peas, fresh or frozen**

Continue cooking until carrots and onions are soft.

Preheat oven to 350° F.

Gravy

Heat to medium heat in a pan:
1/4 cup oil

Stir in and let bubble for about 1 minute:
**3 Tbsp. unbleached white flour   1 tsp. sage
1/2 tsp. black pepper   1/2 tsp. thyme
2 tsp. salt**

Slowly whisk in:
3 cups milk or soymilk

When it begins to boil, add:
**1 tsp. garlic powder
1/2 tsp. paprika**

Pour two-thirds of the gravy over the tofu and vegetables, mix together and pour into the partially baked pie shell. Pour on the rest of the gravy, and cover with a top crust. Seal the edges and cut steam vents. Bake about 30 minutes or until crust is golden.

Per Serving: Calories: 551, Protein: 15 gm., Fat: 38 gm., Carbohydrates: 17 gm.

Manicotti

These manicotti look especially attractive made with home-made spinach noodles.

Have ready:
  **6 cups Italian-Style Tomato Sauce, p. 65,
  or purchased ready-made sauce
  1 (18 oz.) pkg. manicotti noodles or
  one recipe of Noodles or Spinach Noodles, p. 125**

Prepare either Filling No. 1 or No. 2.

Manicotti Filling No. 1

Mash or put through a food mill:
  2 lbs. tofu

Mix in:
  **1/4 cup oil   2 tsp. salt
  2 Tbsp. fresh lemon juice   1/2 tsp. garlic powder
  1 Tbsp. honey or sugar**

Saute together until transparent:
  **1/4 cup oil
  1 1/2 cups onion, chopped**

Mix sauteed onions into tofu mixture along with:
  1 (10 oz.) pkg. frozen spinach, chopped, thawed and drained

Manicotti Filling No. 2

Blend in a blender until smooth and creamy:
  **2 lbs. tofu   2 tsp. salt
  3/4 cup oil   1/2 tsp. garlic powder**

Saute together:
  **2 Tbsp. oil
  1 large onion, chopped fine**

Fold sauteed onions into tofu mixture along with:
  1/2 cup fresh parsley, chopped fine

Drop manicotti noodles into boiling water and boil for about 10 minutes or until noodles are almost "al dente." Rinse and drain. If using home-made noodles, roll the dough out either by machine or by hand to about 1/16" thick. Cut into fourteen 4" x 6" pieces, let them dry for fifteen minutes, then boil the pieces until almost "al dente" (about 3-4 minutes). Rinse, drain, then lay the pieces out on a cloth. Preheat oven to 350° F.

Pour 2 cups of the Italian-Style Tomato Sauce on the bottom of a 9" x 13" pan. Fill each cooked noodle with 1/3-1/2 cup of filling. For the homemade noodles, lay the filling across the shorter end of the noodle and roll it up. Line the filled noodles up in the pan and cover with the rest of the sauce. Bake for about 30 minutes and serve.

Per Serving (No. 1): Calories: 608, Protein: 24 gm., Fat: 22 gm., Carbohydrates: 82 gm.

Per Serving (No. 2): Calories: 688, Protein: 23 gm., Fat: 34 gm., Carbohydrates: 77 gm.

Almond Tofu

Have ready:
1/2 cup roasted almonds

Cut into 3/4" pieces:
2 lbs. firm tofu

Whip together:
1/4 cup soy sauce   **1/4 tsp. garlic powder**
2 Tbsp. peanut butter   **1 tsp. onion powder**

Mix this with the tofu cubes and marinate for 2 hours, stirring occasionally.

Brown the tofu over medium heat until liquid is absorbed in:
2 Tbsp. oil

In another pan, saute together only until crisp-tender:
2 Tbsp. oil   **1 (8 oz.) can water chestnuts, sliced**
1 large bell pepper, cut in 1" squares **1/2 tsp. powdered ginger or**
6-8 green onions, cut in 1 1/2" pieces **1 Tbsp. fresh ginger root, grated**
3 stalks celery, cut in 1" pieces

While the vegetables are cooking, shake together in a jar or blend in a blender:
2 cups cold water   **2 Tbsp. cornstarch**
1/4 cup soy sauce

When the vegetables are crisp-tender, pour the mixture over them and continue simmering until thickened. Add the browned tofu and roasted almonds. Mix well together and serve over rice.

Variation: Replace almonds with roasted cashews for Cashew Tofu.

Per Serving: Calories: 414, Protein: 20 gm., Fat: 36 gm., Carbohydrates: 14 gm.

Almond Tofu

Swiss Steak

Freeze, thaw, squeeze out and slice into 1/4" slices:
3/4 lb. tofu

Marinate for 2 hours or more in a mixture of:
6 Tbsp. soy sauce   **1/4 tsp. pepper**
2 Tbsp. wine vinegar   **1/2 tsp. poultry seasoning**

Dip the marinated tofu in flour, and brown well in:
1/3 cup oil

Turn it once, being careful not to break it up.

Add to the pan:
1 cup onion, sliced
1 cup chopped carrots, celery and/or peppers
1 cup stock (including the remaining marinade)

Cover the pan and cook for 5-10 minutes over a low heat, or until most of the liquid is absorbed. Carefully, turn the tofu again.

Gravy

In a separate pan, bubble together for 2 minutes:
1/4 cup flour, which has been browned
1/4 cup oil

Whip in:
2 Tbsp. soy sauce
1 1/2 cups broth or water

Pour the gravy over the tofu. Cover and cook slowly over low heat for about 1 hour. Serve.

Per Serving: Calories: 427, Protein: 10 gm., Fat: 35 gm., Carbohydrates: 19 gm.

Scrambled Tofu

A fast breakfast dish.

Saute until onions are tender:
3/4 cup onion, chopped
2 Tbsp. oil

Add:
2 lbs. tofu, crumbled   **1/4 tsp. black pepper**
3 Tbsp. soy sauce   **1/4 tsp. garlic powder**
1/4 tsp. salt

Serve hot with toast.

Per Serving: Calories: 140, Protein: 11 gm., Fat: 9 gm., Carbohydrates: 6 gm.

Zucchini Frittata

Serves 4-6
Makes eight 5" frittatas

Saute lightly until tender-crisp:

3 Tbsp. olive oil
1 large onion, sliced thin
4 medium zucchini, sliced thin

1/4 cup fresh parsley, chopped
3 fresh garlic cloves, pressed

Remove from heat.

In a separate bowl, mix together well:

3/4 lb. tofu, blended
1/2 cup tofu, mashed
1 1/2 tsp. salt

3/4 cup flour
2 tsp. baking powder
1 Tbsp. soy sauce

Stir in the sauteed vegetables. Scoop out 1/2 cupfuls of mix on an oiled cookie sheet and flatten into circles. Or oil a large 10" cast iron skillet and fill with all of the mix. Bake for 15 minutes on one side, flip and bake 15 minutes more, or until golden brown. Serve with wide noodles and Tomato Sauce Topping, below.

Tomato Sauce Topping

Makes 2 cups sauce

Mix together in a saucepan:

1 (15 oz.) can tomato sauce
1/4 cup water
1 Tbsp. olive oil
2 tsp. wine vinegar

1/2 tsp. garlic powder
1/2 tsp. salt
3 Tbsp. parsley, chopped fine

Simmer 20 minutes. Spread over frittatas.

Per Serving: Calories: 337, Protein: 13 gm., Fat: 19 gm., Carbohydrates: 32 gm.

Teriyaki Tofu

Serves 6-8

Cut into 1/2" slices:

2 lbs. tofu

Make a marinade of:

1/2 cup soy sauce
2 tsp. honey
2 Tbsp. fresh ginger root, minced

2 cloves garlic, minced
2 Tbsp. vinegar or lemon juice
1 medium onion, diced small

Let tofu slices stand in marinade 2 hours. Drain and reserve marinade. Dip the tofu slices in a mixture of:

1/2 cup unbleached white flour
1/2 tsp. salt
1/4 tsp. black pepper

Brown the floured slices in 1/4 cup oil, adding more as necessary. Reduce heat, pour in reserved marinade and simmer 10 minutes.

Per Serving: Calories: 246, Protein: 12 gm., Fat: 16 gm., Carbohydrates: 16 gm.

Layered Casserole

Serves 8
Makes one 10" spring form pan
or 2 quart souffle dish

Oil the baking dish with 2 tablespoons oil and dust with 2 tablespoons flour. Blend each layer separately and spread evenly into the baking dish. Be careful not to mix the layers.

First layer

Blend together in a blender:
1 lb. tofu
3 cups fresh spinach, chopped,
  cooked and drained or
    1 (10 oz.) pkg. frozen spinach,
    cooked and drained
1/4 cup oil
1 tsp. salt

Second layer

Blend together in a blender:
1 lb. tofu
1/4 cup oil
1 (7 oz.) jar pimentos, chopped
1 tsp. salt
1 Tbsp. lemon juice

Third layer

Blend together in a blender:
1 1/2 lbs. tofu
1/4 cup oil
2 Tbsp. soy sauce
1/4 tsp. garlic powder
1 tsp. salt
1 tsp. onion powder

Fold in:
1 cup fresh mushrooms, chopped in 1/4" pieces

Bake at 350° F. for 1 hour or until set. Let stand and cool a few minutes before serving. Can be served hot or cold.

Per Serving: Calories: 375, Protein: 17 gm., Fat: 32 gm., Carbohydrates: 8 gm.

Layered Casserole

Chinese Sweet and Sour Balls

Serves 6
Makes thirty-six 2" balls

Mash in a bowl:
 1 1/2 lbs. tofu

Mix in:

 1 1/2 Tbsp. peanut butter
 3 Tbsp. soy sauce
 1/4 cup parsley
 8 green onions,
  cut in 1/4" pieces

 1 (8 oz.) can water chestnuts, chopped
 1/4 cup mushrooms,
  sliced (canned) or 1/2 cup fresh
 1 cup green peppers,
  cut in 1/4" pieces

Form 2" balls, roll in flour and fry in 1/2" oil, browning on all sides. Do not let the oil smoke. Drain on absorbent paper. Serve hot on rice with Sweet and Sour Sauce, below.

Sweet and Sour Sauce

Combine in a saucepan over medium heat:

 1 1/2 cups unsweetened pineapple juice
 1/2 cup plus 2 Tbsp. brown sugar
 1/2 cup apple cider vinegar

 1/4 tsp. garlic powder
 2 Tbsp. cornstarch
 1/4 cup soy sauce

Whisk out all lumps and heat, stirring constantly until thickened.

Per Serving: Calories: 278, Protein: 12 gm., Fat: 7 gm., Carbohydrates: 46 gm.

Sweet and Sour Tofu

Serves 4-6

Cut into small cubes (about 1/2"):
 1 lb. firm tofu

Mix the cubes together with a mixture of:

 1/4 cup soy sauce
 1/4 cup bouillon or water
 1/2 tsp. salt

 1/2 cup cornstarch
  (or 1/4 cup cornstarch and 1/4 cup flour)

Deep-fry the cubes in oil at 350° F., being sure the cubes separate in the oil. Remove when golden brown (about 2-3 minutes). Drain and serve with Sweet and Sour Sauce, above, poured over.

Per Serving: Calories: 366, Protein: 9 gm., Fat: 13 gm., Carbohydrates: 57 gm.

Chinese Sweet and Sour Balls

Spring Rolls

Spring Rolls can be served as main dish or an appetizer if made in a smaller size.

Have ready:
   ready-made eggroll wrappers

Prepare Spring Roll Filling No. 1 or No. 2.

Spring Roll Filling No. 1

Makes thirty-six 2" x 3" rolls

Cut into 1" x 1/2" x 1/4" strips:
   3/4 lb. tofu

Marinate these for 2 hours in a mixture of:

1 Tbsp. peanut butter	**1 tsp. wine vinegar**
3 Tbsp. soy sauce	**1/4 tsp. garlic powder**
1 Tbsp. ginger root, grated	

In a wok or large skillet, stir-fry until crisp-tender:

2 Tbsp. oil	**6 large green onions,**
1 1/2 cups Chinese cabbage,	**cut in 1/2" pieces**
shredded fine	**1/2 cup fresh mushrooms, sliced**
1/2 cup celery, chopped fine	**1 Tbsp. soy sauce**
1/2 cup water chestnuts, chopped fine	

In a separate skillet, brown the marinated tofu in:
   2 Tbsp. oil

Add any leftover marinade while browning. Mix tofu and vegetables together.

Spring Roll Filling No. 2

Makes sixteen 2" x 3" rolls

Heat in a wok or heavy skillet:
   1 Tbsp. oil

Add:
   1 tsp. ginger root, peeled and minced
   2 cloves garlic

Cook 1 minute and remove. To the same pan add:
   1 lb. tofu, crumbled

Stir and add:
   2 Tbsp. soy sauce
   1/2 tsp. sugar

Stir and remove from pan. Add to the same pan and stir-fry for 5 minutes:
   1 Tbsp. oil
   4 cups celery, diced

Add and stir in:
   1/2 lb. fresh mung bean sprouts

(Spring Rolls, continued on next page)

(Spring Rolls, continued)

Add the tofu mixture, stir, then pour in the center of the pan a mixture of:

1 Tbsp. cornstarch   **2 Tbsp. water**

Cook until thickened. Remove from heat.

To prepare each Spring Roll, place 1/4-1/3 cup filling in the center of each wrapper. Tuck the bottom corner around the filling, then fold the side corners in. Roll it over, securing the top flap to the roll with a dab of water. Deep-fry **3** or **4** at a time in 350° F. oil until golden brown, turning to brown both sides. Drain on absorbent paper and serve hot with Sweet and Sour Sauce, p. 76, or mustard or soy sauce.

Per Roll (No. 1): Calories: 245, Protein: 7 gm., Fat: 22 gm., Carbohydrates: 8 gm.

Per Roll (No. 2): Calories: 250, Protein: 9 gm., Fat: 20 gm., Carbohydrates: 11 gm.

Onion Pie

Serves 6
Makes one 13" pizza pan

Crust

Dissolve together in a large mixing bowl:
1 cup warm water   **1 Tbsp. honey**
1 (1 Tbsp.) pkg. active dry yeast

Let rise 10 minutes, then add:
4 cups unbleached white flour   **1 tsp. salt**

Mix together well, cover with a cloth and let rise in a warm place for 1/2 hour.

Filling

Saute together:
1/4 cup oil
5 medium onions, cut in 1/4" rings (about 4 cups)

Remove from heat when transparent.

Blend in a blender until smooth and creamy:
1/2 lb. tofu   **1 clove garlic**
1/4 cup oil   **2 Tbsp. vinegar**
1 Tbsp. soy sauce

Mix this together with the sauteed onions.

Preheat oven to 400° F.

Sprinkle a board with cornmeal, then roll the crust dough into a circle to fit the pizza pan, leaving a lip around the edge. Spread the filling on the dough, as for pizza. Bake for about 25 minutes, or until crust is golden.

Variation: For Carrot Pie substitute 1/2 cup chopped onion and 4 cups grated carrots for the onions rings.

Per Serving: Calories: 579, Protein: 15 gm., Fat: 20 gm., Carbohydrates: 81 gm.

Korean Barbecue Tofu

Serves 6

Cut into 1/4" slices:
1 1/2 lbs. firm tofu

Marinate at least 2 hours (overnight is best) in a mixture of:
1/2 cup soy sauce
6 Tbsp. sugar
2 tsp. dry mustard
4 cloves garlic, minced fine or
 1/2 tsp. garlic powder
2 tsp. onion powder

Brown on both sides in:
2 Tbsp. oil.

Garnish with chopped green onion and serve with rice. Can top with mushrooms and snow peas.

Per Serving: Calories: 187, Protein: 10 gm., Fat: 9 gm., Carbohydrates: 18 gm.

Marinating Korean Barbecue with the help of a baster

Tofu and Broccoli in Garlic Sauce   *Serves 6*

Cut into cubes:
1 1/2 lbs. tofu

Marinate in:
1/4 cup soy sauce

Carefully stir the marinating tofu occasionally while preparing the sauce.

Cut in half lengthwise, then into thin half-rings and set aside:
2 medium onions

Slice and set aside:
8 oz. fresh mushrooms

Crush and set aside:
1 bud garlic, (medium size, 8-10 cloves)

Cut into large flowerettes and set aside:
1 lb. broccoli

Dissolve together and set aside:
2 cups boiling water
2 cubes vegetable bouillon

Drain the tofu and reserve liquid. Brown tofu in a heavy skillet or wok on all sides in:
1/2 cup oil

Remove tofu when brown.

Add to the pan:
1 Tbsp. oil

Quickly fry the onions and mushrooms until soft.

Add and stir together:
the crushed garlic   **1 tsp. crushed red pepper**
the bouillon mixture   **(more or less to taste)**
1 Tbsp. prepared Chinese mustard   **1/4 tsp. ginger**
3 Tbsp. honey

Add:
the tofu and reserved marinade

Simmer over medium heat for 1 minute, then add:
the cut broccoli

Simmer 3 minutes more. Turn off and set aside for 5 minutes. Serve over rice.

Per Serving: Calories: 337, Protein: 12 gm., Fat: 25 gm., Carbohydrates: 22 gm.

Tofu Knishes

These can be made smaller to be served as appetizers.

Have ready:
2 1/2 cups cooked potatoes, peeled and mashed

Dough

Beat together:
1 cup potatoes, mashed
1 Tbsp. oil
1 tsp. salt

Add:
3 cups unbleached white flour
1 tsp. baking powder

Mix well, then mix in:
1/2 cup cold water

Knead into a smooth dough, then let rest on a board, covered with a cloth, for 1/2 hour.

Filling

Saute until transparent:
2 Tbsp. oil
1 cup onions, chopped

Mix together with:
1 1/2 cups potatoes, mashed   **1/4 tsp. black pepper**
1 1/2 cups tofu, mashed   **1/2 tsp. garlic powder**
1 tsp. salt   **1/4 cup fresh parsley, chopped**

Cut the dough into 4 sections, then roll each section as thin as possible (about 1/16" thick). Cut into 5" x 6" rectangles. Place 2 or 3 tablespoons of filling in the middle of each rectangle. Fold sides in first, then the ends.

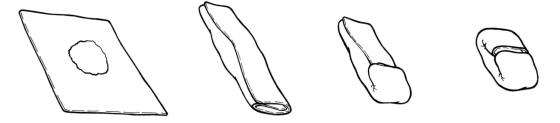

Place folded side down on an oiled cookie sheet. Bake for 25 minutes or until golden. Serve with horseradish or mustard.

Per Serving: Calories: 433, Protein: 13 gm., Fat: 12 gm., Carbohydrates: 57 gm.

Basic Fried Tofu

Serves 4-6

Cut into slices 1/4" to 1/2" thick:
1 1/2 lbs. firm tofu

Fry on both sides on an oiled griddle or skillet until lightly browned. While they are frying, sprinkle with:
soy sauce or salt to taste
garlic powder to taste

These can be served as part of a sandwich or with rice, noodles or toast as part of any meal or snack.

Variation: Spread the tofu slices with a thin layer of Marmite* and fry. Thinly sliced frozen tofu (which has been thawed and squeezed out) is also very tasty done this way.

*Marmite is a popular salty-yeast spread in Canada and Great Britain. It can be found in the special foods section of a supermarket.

Per Serving: Calories: 200, Protein: 11 gm., Fat: 17 gm., Carbohydrates: 4 gm.

Quiche

Serves 4-6
Makes one 8" pie

Preheat oven to 350° F.

Have ready:
1 unbaked 8" pie shell

Saute together:
6 Tbsp. oil
1 medium onion, chopped

When soft, add to:
1 1/2 lbs. tofu, mashed
1 1/2 Tbsp. soy sauce
1 Tbsp. dry mustard
1 tsp. salt

1/2 tsp. garlic powder
1/4 tsp. black pepper
3 Tbsp. lemon juice

Mix well. Pour tofu mixture into pie shell. Bake for 45-60 minutes until set.

Variation: Cover the bottom of an unbaked pie shell with 3/4 cup crumbled fried tempeh* which has been drained, or 1/2 cup imitation bacon bits, then fill with the tofu mixture and bake.

*Tempeh is a cultured soyfood made by incubating partially cooked split soybeans. Tempeh is available in a few health food stores.

Per Serving: Calories: 433, Protein: 13 gm., Fat: 34 gm., Carbohydrates: 6 gm.

Quiche

Jewish-Style Stuffed Cabbage Rolls

Serves 6

Have ready:
1 cup cooked rice

Sauce

Mix and simmer in a large saucepan while preparing filling:

1 (6 oz.) can tomato paste
7 cups water
1/4 cup raisins

1 Tbsp. salt
6 Tbsp. sugar
2 Tbsp. lemon juice

Filling

Saute together until limp:

3 Tbsp. oil
1 medium onion, chopped

1 clove garlic, chopped

Turn off heat and mix in:

1 1/2 lbs. tofu, mashed
1 cup cooked rice

2 Tbsp. soy sauce
1 tsp. salt

Wash 18 large cabbage leaves and put each leaf into boiling water for 1-2 minutes to soften. (It's all right to boil 3-4 at a time.) Drain and trim out the hard center core strip. Put 2-3 tablespoons of filling on each leaf, fold the sides in and roll up. You can use toothpicks to hold them together if needed. Carefully drop the rolls into simmering sauce and don't stir so they won't fall apart. Simmer 2-3 hours, not stirring, but pushing down on the top rolls occasionally. Can be served as they are or over mashed potatoes or rice.

Per Serving: Calories: 331, Protein: 14 gm., Fat: 12 gm., Carbohydrates: 41 gm.

Oven-Fried Tofu

Serves 6

Preheat oven to 375° F.

Cut into 1/2″ slices:
2 lbs. firm tofu

Mix together in a bowl:

1 1/4 cups unbleached white flour
2 Tbsp. onion powder
2 tsp. chili powder
2 tsp. salt

2 tsp. garlic powder
1 tsp. dried parsley flakes
1/4 tsp. black pepper

In another bowl, mix together:

3 Tbsp. soy sauce

1 1/2 Tbsp. water

Generously oil a cookie sheet. Dip each slice of tofu into the soy sauce mixture, then into the flour mixture, then place it on the oiled cookie sheet. Bake at 375° F. for about 15 minutes on each side or until each side is browned. Add more oil to the cookie sheet when you flip the pieces. Serve as they are or in sandwiches.

Per Serving: Calories: 285, Protein: 15 gm., Fat: 14 gm., Carbohydrates: 26 gm.

Tofu Mushroom Roll

Filling

Saute together:
1 Tbsp. oil
6 oz. mushrooms, chopped

In another pan, saute until transparent:
2 Tbsp. oil
3/4 cup onions, chopped

Set aside 1/3 of the onions for the sauce.

Fry lightly in another pan:

2 Tbsp. oil	**3/4 tsp. thyme**
1 1/2 lbs. tofu, crumbled	**1/4 tsp. black pepper**
1 tsp. salt	**1/3 cup parsley, minced**

Add the sauteed mushrooms and 1/2 cup onions to this and mix well. Set aside.

Dough

Mix together:
3 cup unbleached white flour
4 1/2 tsp. baking powder
1 tsp. salt

Pour in and mix:
1/2 cup oil

Pour in:
1 scant cup cold water

Stir together to form a ball. Roll out 1/3" to 1/2" thick on a well-floured board into an oblong shape. Spread on the filling, being careful not to tear the dough. Roll it up lengthwise and seal the edge with water. Place on an oiled cookie sheet and cut slits in the top. Brush lightly with oil and bake at 400° F. for 25-30 minutes until lightly browned.

Sauce

Lightly saute:
2 Tbsp. oil
12 oz. fresh mushrooms, sliced

In another pan, bubble together over low heat for 1 minute:
1/4 cup oil
1/2 cup unbleached white flour

Stir in:
4 cup stock or bouillon

Cook until thickened (it will be a thin sauce). Stir in mushrooms and reserved 1/4 cup sauteed onions. Pour over slices of the roll and serve.

Per Serving: Calories: 686, Protein: 16 gm., Fat: 44 gm., Carbohydrates: 56 gm.

Falafels

Have ready:
   6-8 purchased pita breads
   2 cups dried chickpeas (garbanzo beans)

Cook 2 cups dried beans or use 4 cups canned beans. Reserve the cooking water or juice in the cans.

Blend together in a blender until creamy:
   4 cups chickpeas, drained
   1 cup chickpea cooking water
   3 cloves fresh garlic

Pour this into a mixing bowl and add:
   1 lb. tofu, mashed
   1/3 cup soy sauce
   1 tsp. salt
   1/4 tsp. black pepper
   1 medium onion, chopped fine
   6 cups whole grain bread crumbs

Mix together until all ingredients are moist. Form 2″ balls and roll in unbleached white flour. Fry the balls in 1/2″ oil at 350° F., turning each one until golden all around.

Cut pita breads in half and open pockets carefully. Pita breads can be warmed up in a moderate oven for a few minutes, but should remain soft. Put 3-4 balls in each pocket. Pour 2-3 tablespoons (more if you like) Tahini Sauce, below, over the balls and top with chopped tomatoes and lettuce.

Tahini Sauce

Blend in a blender until creamy:
   1/2 cup tahini* (sesame butter)
   1/4 cup olive oil
   1/4 cup vegetable oil
   1/4 cup lemon juice (juice of about 1 1/2 lemons)
   2 cloves fresh garlic
   2 Tbsp. soy sauce or
   1 1/2 Tbsp. tamari soy sauce*

This may be served warmed up or cold. It will keep up to 2 weeks in the refrigerator and is also good on salads, fried tofu, or noodles.

*If you cannot find these in a special foods section of a supermarket, you could try a health food or natural food store.

Per Serving: Calories: 987, Protein: 37 gm., Fat: 40 gm., Carbohydrates: 101 gm.

Sloppy Joes

An All-American dish featuring tofu.

Saute until tender:
  3 Tbsp. oil
  1 large onion, diced
  2 medium green peppers, diced

Add:

  3 cups tomato sauce
  1 1/2 Tbsp. chili powder
  (more if you like)
  1 tsp. salt

  1/8 tsp. black pepper
  1 Tbsp. soy sauce
  1 Tbsp. salad mustard
  1 Tbsp. sugar

Simmer together over low heat for about 20 minutes.

Brown in another skillet:
  3 Tbsp. oil
  1 1/2 lbs. firm tofu, grated or crumbled
  4 Tbsp. Worcestershire sauce or
  1 Tbsp. Kitchen Bouquet

When the tofu is well browned and has absorbed the flavoring, add the tomato sauce and serve over sandwich buns.

Variation: For Sloppy Joe Turnovers prepare Turnover Dough, p. 93, and follow directions for making the turnovers, using the Sloppy Joe mix for the filling.

Per Serving: Calories: 457, Protein: 17 gm., Fat: 8 gm., Carbohydrates: 28 gm.

Vegetable Chow Yuk

In a wok or skillet, fry over medium low heat until all sides are browned:
  1/4 cup oil
  1 1/2 lbs. tofu, cut in 1 1/2" cubes

Add:

  1 medium onion, sliced
  6 stalks celery, cut in 1" diagonal slices

  6 green onions, cut in half lengthwise
  2 large bell peppers, sliced

Cover and simmer for 5 minutes, stirring several times.

Mix together well:
  1/2 cup water
  1/3 cup soy sauce

  2 Tbsp. sugar
  1/2 tsp. garlic powder

Pour over the tofu and vegetables. Cover and cook another 10 minutes.

In the last five minutes of cooking add and stir in:
  2 cups fresh mung bean sprouts
  1/2 lb. fresh mushrooms, sliced

Serve over hot rice.

Per Serving: Calories: 223, Protein: 12 gm., Fat: 14 gm., Carbohydrates: 15 gm.

Tofu Turnovers

These are good hot or cold, for lunchboxes or picnics, and can be frozen and reheated later.

Turnover Dough

Stir together in a large mixing bowl:
   1 1/2 cups potato water, warm
   1/2 cup potatoes, mashed
   1 Tbsp. active dry yeast
   1 Tbsp. sugar

Let rise 10 minutes. Then mix in gradually:
   7-8 cups unbleached white flour
   1 1/2 tsp. salt
   1/4 cup oil

Knead the dough until smooth and not sticky. Divide into 18 balls about 2" in diameter. Roll each one out on a floured board into a 6" circle or roll the dough out 1/8" thick and cut into 6" squares. Put 2-3 tablespoons Turnover Filling, below, in the center of each circle (or square) of rolled out dough. Moisten the edges with water, fold over and seal by pressing together the edges with a fork.

Bake at 425° F. for about 15 minutes or until lightly browned. Be careful, they burn easily. Serve in a cloth-lined basket.

Turnover Filling

Saute together for about 10 minutes:
   2 Tbsp. oil
   1 lb. tofu, mashed
   2 Tbsp. soy sauce
   3 stalks celery, chopped in 1/4" pieces
   3 medium carrots, sliced thin
   1 medium onion, chopped
   3/4 cup snow peas or
    early peas (fresh or frozen)
   3 cloves garlic, minced
   1 small green pepper, cut in 1/4" pieces
   1 tsp. salt

Turn off heat and add:
   1/2 lb. tofu, blended

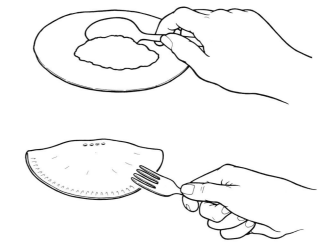

Per Serving: Calories: 230, Protein: 9 gm., Fat: 16 gm., Carbohydrates: 10 gm.

Taquitos

Serves 6

Crispy little tacos served with Avocado Sauce.

Have ready:
24 corn tortillas

Freeze, thaw, squeeze dry and tear into bite-size pieces:
1 1/2 lbs. tofu

Avocado Sauce

Peel and mash:
2 ripe avocados

Stir in:
1 cup green taco sauce
(more if you like it hotter)
1 tsp. garlic powder

Chill for one hour before serving.

Filling

Mix together:
3 Tbsp. soy sauce
2 Tbsp. peanut butter
6 cloves garlic, pressed

Work this mixture into the bite-sized tofu pieces, then mix in:
1 cup onion, diced

Brown the whole mixture in:
1/4 cup oil

Set aside.

Soften the tortillas either by dipping each one with tongs into 350° F. oil for 1-2 seconds or spread the tortillas out on a cookie sheet and put in a preheated 350° F. oven for about 2 minutes. The tortillas need to be soft and flexible to roll easily.

Lay 2-2 1/2 tablespoons of filling across each tortilla and wrap the tortilla snugly around the filling. Insert a wooden toothpick through each end and in the middle of each one to keep it closed.

Taquitos can then be either pan-fried or oven-fried. Pan-fry 3 at a time in a heavy skillet with 3/4" oil heated to 350° F. When golden brown on one side, turn over to fry until golden brown on the other side. Then drain. To oven-fry, lay the rolled taquitos on an oiled cookie sheet, then put in a preheated 350° F. oven for 8-10 minutes on each side or until crisp.

Remove the toothpicks and serve with Avocado Sauce. These can also be served with refried pinto beans, Spanish Rice and tossed green salad.

Per Serving: Calories: 716, Protein: 22 gm., Fat: 50 gm., Carbohydrates: 52 gm.

Won Ton

Won Ton may be deep-fried or boiled. This recipe makes 85-90 won ton, which uses up one package of won ton wrappers. Deep-fried as a main dish, this will serve 8 or 10. If you are using them in soup you may want only 3 or 4 for a serving. See p. 22 for Watercress Soup with Won Ton. The excess may be frozen and cooked later.

Have ready:
  1 package won ton wrappers

Filling

Stir-fry together about 2 minutes in a wok or heavy skillet:
  2 Tbsp. oil   **1/4 cup celery, chopped**
  1 Tbsp. ginger root, peeled and minced   **1 lb. tofu, crumbled fine**
  1 cup Chinese cabbage, chopped   **1 Tbsp. soy sauce**
  1 cup fresh bean sprouts

There are many ways to fold a won ton. Your won ton package will show you some variations. One way is to start with a square and place one teaspoon of filling in the middle of the square. Fold the wrapper in half diagonally to form a triangle, then fold it in half again, forming a long trapezoidal shape. Bring the longest ends together, then press and stick them together with a dab of water. This will form a pointed tail on the won ton.

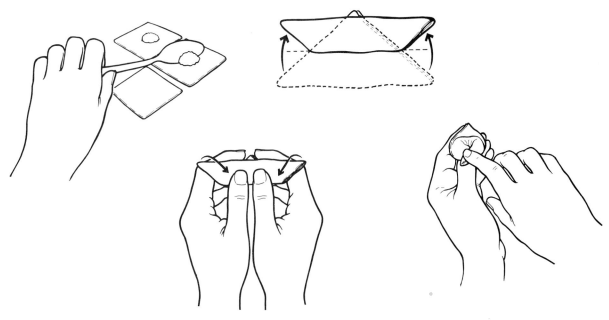

Another way is to cut your won ton wrappers into circles. This can be done several at a time with scissors or a sharp knife. Place one teaspoon of filling in the lower half of the circle. Fold the top half over and seal with a dab of water. Take the two corners of the resulting half-circle and bring them around to meet each other, pressing them together with a dab of water to make them stick.

Deep-fry won ton in 350° F. oil until golden brown. Drain and serve or boil won ton in boiling water or soup for the last 5 minutes of cooking.

Per Serving: Calories: 218, Protein: 6 gm., Fat: 15 gm., Carbohydrates: 15 gm.

Stewart's Stew

Combine in a 5-quart saucepan and boil until vegetables are almost soft:

2 1/2 qts. water   **4 medium onions, chopped**
5 medium potatoes, chopped   **1/2 tsp. salt**
6 carrots, chopped

Meanwhile, cut into 3/4" cubes and marinate for 15 minutes:
1 1/2 lbs. tofu
1/2 cup soy sauce

Drain soy sauce into cooking vegetables.

Combine in a bag:
1 cup unbleached white flour
1 tsp. salt
1 tsp. black pepper

Shake to mix up, then add marinated tofu cubes. Brown the breaded cubes in:
1/2 cup oil

Be careful not to knock off the breading when turning the cubes. Add the browned cubes to the almost soft vegetables. Mix any leftover breading into a smooth paste with a little broth, then add to the stew. Continue boiling until the vegetables are soft.

Per Serving: Calories: 395, Protein: 14 gm., Fat: 20 gm., Carbohydrates: 42 gm.

Tofu Paprika

Cut into 1/2" slices and lightly fry:
1 lb. tofu
1/4 cup oil

Sprinkle while frying with:
1/2 tsp. salt
2 tsp. garlic powder or 2 cloves garlic, minced

Remove tofu from the pan. To the same pan add:

3 Tbsp. oil   **4 cups onions, thinly sliced**
1/2 tsp. salt   **(about 4 large onions)**

Lightly brown the onions and return the tofu to the pan.

Sprinkle with:
1 1/2 Tbsp. paprika

Add to the pan:
1 cup bouillon broth or water

Cover and simmer 10 minutes, then add:
2 1/2 cups (double recipe) Tofu Sour Creme Dressing, p. 41

When sauce is heated through, serve on rice, noodles or mashed potatoes.

Per Serving: Calories: 560, Protein: 16 gm., Fat: 49 gm., Carbohydrates: 19 gm.

Eggplant Sandwiches

Makes 8-10

Have ready:
1/2 recipe Ricotta-Style Filling, p. 59

Peel and cut into sixteen to twenty 1/2" slices:
1 medium-size eggplant

Cover the slices in cold water and soak for 10 minutes with:
1 tsp. salt

Breading

Mix together:

1 1/4 cups unbleached white flour	**dash of black pepper**
1/2 cup cornmeal	**1/2 tsp. salt**
2 medium cloves garlic, crushed	**1 tsp. oregano flakes**

Dry the eggplant slices on paper towels, then dredge each eggplant slice in breading. Place on a cookie sheet which has been spread with:
2 Tbsp. oil

Oven-fry at 350° F. for about 8-10 minutes or until golden brown.

Turn over and brown the other side, adding:
2 Tbsp. oil

Spread half the slices with 1/4-1/3 cup Ricotta-Style Filling on each side, add a slice of ripe tomato and sprouts, then top with a second eggplant slice. Serve.

Per Serving: Calories: 529, Protein: 21 gm., Fat: 33 gm., Carbohydrates: 40 gm.

Crunchy Tofu Cutlets or Sticks

Serves 6

Preheat oven to 400° F.

Freeze, thaw, and squeeze out:
2 lbs. tofu

Or have ready:
2 lbs. firm tofu

Cut the tofu into 1 1/2" x 3" x 3/4" pieces and marinate for 2 hours in:
1/4 cup soy sauce

Dip each stick in oil, then roll in a mixture of:

1 cup cracker crumbs	**1 tsp. garlic powder**
1 cup unbleached white flour	**2 tsp. parsley flakes**
1 tsp. salt	**1/2 tsp. turmeric**

Brush a cookie sheet with:
2 Tbsp. oil

Lay the tofu pieces on the cookie sheet leaving about 1/2" between each piece. Bake for 15 minutes on each side. Serve with Tartare Sauce, p. 42, or cocktail sauce.

Per Serving: Calories: 256, Protein: 15 gm., Fat: 11 gm., Carbohydrates: 24 gm.

Side Dishes

Clockwise from top right: Stuffed Baked Tomatoes,
Risotto Verde and Tofu Fried Rice

SIDE DISHES

Risotto Verde

Serves 6-8

Preheat oven to 325° F.

Have ready:
  2 cups cooked rice

Thaw and reserve liquid:
  1 (10 oz.) pkg. of chopped frozen spinach

Blend until smooth and creamy:
  1/2 lb. tofu
  2 Tbsp. oil
  2 Tbsp. spinach juice (from thawing)
  1 1/2 tsp. salt

Saute:
  2 Tbsp. oil
  1 medium onion, finely chopped
  2 cloves garlic, minced

Remove from heat and fold in:
  the cooked rice
  1/4 tsp. freshly ground black pepper
  1/8 tsp. nutmeg
  the thawed spinach
  the blended tofu mixture

Bake in an oiled 1 1/2-quart glass baking dish for 30 minutes.

Variation: Substitute 1/2 cup fresh chopped parsley for the spinach and leave out the nutmeg.

Per Serving: Calories: 194, Protein: 6 gm., Fat: 12 gm., Carbohydrates: 19 gm.

Java Tofu Pilaf

Serves 6-8

Cut into cubes:
1 1/2 lbs. firm tofu

Mix together until smooth:
1/4 cup soy sauce
2 Tbsp. peanut butter

Pour over the tofu cubes and mix together.

Brown the cubes in:
3 Tbsp. oil

In another skillet, saute:
1/4 cup oil
1 large onion, chopped

When the onion pieces become limp add:

2 1/2 Tbsp. curry powder   **·2 1/2 tsp. salt**
1/2 tsp. coriander   **1 cup uncooked rice**
1/2 tsp. cumin   **1/2 cup raisins**

Mix all together and toast 5 minutes.

Then pour in:
3 1/2 cups boiling water
the browned tofu

Mix, bring to a boil, stir, cover, turn heat to low and simmer 20 minutes. Serve.

Per Serving: Calories: 360, Protein: 12 gm., Fat: 20 gm., Carbohydrates: 22 gm.

Stuffed Baked Tomatoes

Serves 8-12

Wash 8 large or 12 small ripe tomatoes, then cut or scoop out a hollow on the stem end, leaving about 2/3-3/4 of the tomato.

Stuffing

Saute together until soft:
2 Tbsp. oil
1 cup onion, diced
1/2 cup green pepper, diced

Preheat oven to 400° F.

Mix together in a bowl:

1 lb. tofu, mashed   **1 Tbsp. soy sauce**
1/4 cup parsley, chopped fine   **1/4 tsp. garlic powder**

Combine sauteed vegetables and tofu mixture. Stuff tomatoes and arrange in a 9″ square oiled baking pan. Top with bread or cracker crumbs. Bake for 20 minutes. Serve hot or chilled.

Per Serving: Calories: 105, Protein: 5 gm., Fat: 6 gm., Carbohydrates: 9 gm.

Tofu Kartoffelkuchen

This also makes a good breakfast.

Mix together:
 8 medium potatoes, grated
 1/2 lb. tofu, blended
 1 large onion, grated
 1/4 cup fresh parsley, chopped fine
 1 tsp. salt
 1/4 tsp. black pepper
 1/2 tsp. garlic powder
 3 Tbsp. unbleached white flour

For each pancake, brush a 6" skillet with oil and heat to medium heat. Spoon about 3/4 cup of the potato mixture into the pan and flatten to 3/8"-1/2" thick. Fry about 5-7 minutes on each side or until golden brown. Serve hot with applesauce on the side, or top with Tofu Sour Creme Dressing, p. 41.

Per Serving: Calories: 266, Protein: 8 gm., Fat: 11 gm., Carbohydrates: 36 gm.

Tofu Kartoffelkuchen

Walnut-Stuffed Zucchini

Serves 4-6

Preheat oven to 375° F.

Wash and trim the ends off:
4 small zucchini

Cut the zucchini in half lengthwise, scoop out the seed pulp and set aside. Parboil the shells for 1 minute and drain.

Saute together until transparent:
2 Tbsp. oil
1/3 cup onion, chopped

Beat together with an electric mixer:

3/4 lb. tofu	**1 tsp. salt**
2 Tbsp. oil	**1 tsp. sugar**
2 Tbsp. vinegar	**1/8 tsp. black pepper**

Chop the zucchini pulp and mix it together with sauteed onions and the tofu mixture.

Stir in:
1/2 cup walnuts, chopped

Heap onto shells. Sprinkle with paprika. Bake on an oiled sheet for 15-20 minutes.

Per Serving: Calories: 253, Protein: 8 gm., Fat: 22 gm., Carbohydrates: 9 gm.

Spinach Souffle

Serves 6

Preheat oven to 350° F.

Thaw:
1 (10 oz.) package frozen chopped spinach, reserving juice.

Saute until limp:
3 Tbsp. oil
1/2 cup onion, chopped

Stir in:

3 Tbsp. flour	**1/2 tsp. salt**
1 cup liquid (including spinach juice and water, milk or soymilk)	**dash of freshly ground black pepper**
	dash of nutmeg

Fold spinach into sauce.

Blend until smooth and creamy:

1 cup tofu	**2 Tbsp. fresh lemon juice or vinegar**
2 Tbsp. oil	**dash of freshly ground black pepper**
1 tsp. salt	

Fold into spinach and sauce. Bake in oiled 8" round pan or 8" square pan for 30 minutes.

Per Serving: Calories: 184, Protein: 5 gm., Fat: 16 gm., Carbohydrates: 8 gm.

Tofu Rice Ring

Have ready:
4 cups cooked rice
Whip together:
1/4 cup soy sauce
2 Tbsp. peanut butter
1/4 tsp. garlic powder
1 tsp. onion powder

Pour this over:
1 lb. tofu, cut into 1/2" cubes

Mix carefully until all cubes are coated.

Brown the cubes in:
2 Tbsp. oil

Saute together in another pan:
1 Tbsp. oil
1 large stalk celery, diced
4 green onions, cut in 1/2" pieces

Preheat oven to 400° F.

Add sauteed vegetables and tofu to:
4 cups cooked rice
1 cup black olives, pitted and sliced
1/4 cup pimentos, chopped

Stir gently, then add:
1/2 cup blended tofu
1/8 tsp. black pepper

Stir gently again until just blended. Press firmly into a well-oiled 5-6 cup ring mold. Fit the ring mold inside another baking pan which has 1" of water in the bottom, and bake for 20 minutes. Remove from the oven and let cool 5 minutes. Loosen the edges with a knife and turn out onto a platter. Serve with the center of the ring filled with steamed vegetables.

Per Serving: Calories: 382, Protein: 11 gm., Fat: 14 gm., Carbohydrates: 54 gm.

Stuffed Zucchini

Wash and remove stems from:
6 medium zucchini

Steam for 5 minutes. Cut in half and scoop out seeds. Reserve for filling. Arrange the zucchini in an oiled baking dish.

Cut into 1/2" cubes:
1 lb. firm tofu

Marinate the cubes for 2 hours in a mixture of:
1/4 cup soy sauce
2 Tbsp. peanut butter

Brown in:
2 Tbsp. oil

In another pan, saute until crisp-tender:
2 Tbsp. oil
1 cup onions, chopped
1 cup celery, chopped
1 1/2 cups fresh mushrooms, sliced
the zucchini pulp, chopped
1 clove garlic, minced

Add to this:
1/2 cup whole grain bread crumbs
the marinated tofu

Stuff this mixture into the zucchini shells.

In a saucepan, simmer together for 10 minutes:
1 (6 oz.) can tomato paste
4 cans water
1 clove garlic, minced
1/2 tsp. oregano
1/4 tsp. basil
1 small bay leaf
1 tsp. salt
2 tsp. honey or sugar
1/4 tsp. black pepper

Preheat oven to 350° F.

Remove the bay leaf and pour the tomato sauce over the stuffed zucchini. Bake for about 25 minutes.

Per Serving: Calories: 227, Protein: 7 gm., Fat: 14 gm., Carbohydrates: 23 gm.

Chiliquiles

Cut or tear into bite-size pieces:
2 dozen corn tortillas

Mix together and set aside:
1/2 lb. tofu, crumbled
1 (8 oz.) jar picante sauce
3 small cloves garlic, pressed

Heat in a large skillet or wok:
1/4 cup oil

When hot (don't let it smoke) add:
the cut-up tortillas

Stir-fry over medium heat until the pieces are coated with oil.

Add:
1 medium onion, chopped

Stir-fry until the tortilla pieces are golden brown.

Sprinkle with:
1 1/2 tsp. salt

Add the tofu-picante sauce mixture to the pan and mix well. Cover and steam 2-3 minutes.

Add, stirring constantly:
1/4 cup oil

Stir-fry a few minutes more and serve.

Per Serving: Calories: 362, Protein: 10 gm., Fat: 24 gm., Carbohydrates: 32 gm.

Chiliquiles

Tofu Fried Rice

Have ready:
4 cups cooked rice, cooled

Heat in a heavy skillet or wok:
2 Tbsp. oil
2 cloves garlic, crushed

Cook until garlic is light brown, then remove and discard the garlic.

Add and stir-fry for 1 minute:
3/4 lb. tofu, diced

Add and stir in well:
1 Tbsp. soy sauce

Remove tofu from pan. Add to the pan:
2 Tbsp. oil
2 cloves garlic, minced

Let fry for 1 minute. Then add:
1 1/2 cups onion, diced
1 cup celery, diced

Stir-fry for 2-3 minutes. Then add:
the cooked rice
1/2 Tbsp. oil
1/2 tsp. salt

Stir-fry until everything has some oil on it. Then add:
the diced and fried tofu
1 1/2 cups fresh bean sprouts

Stir-fry 2 minutes. Then add:
1 Tbsp. soy sauce

Mix well. Serve hot, topped with chopped green onion.

Per Serving: Calories: 271, Protein: 8 gm., Fat: 11 gm., Carbohydrates: 36 gm.

Corn Pie

A South-of-the-Border casserole.

Preheat oven to 350° F.

Saute together until onions are transparent:
2 Tbsp. oil
1 medium onion, chopped

Add and fry for 5 minutes more:
3/4 lb. tofu, crumbled
1 tsp. salt
1 tsp. chili powder
1/4 tsp. black pepper
2 dashes cayenne

Stir in:
1 (17 oz.) can cut corn, drained or
2 cups frozen whole kernel corn
18 black olives, pitted and cut in half
1/2 cup water

Pour into an oiled 6 1/2" x 10" pan.

Mix together in a bowl:
3/4 cup corn meal
1/4 cup unbleached white flour
1 Tbsp. sugar
1 tsp. baking powder
1/2 tsp. salt
1/4 tsp. baking soda

Pour into the flour mixture:
3/4 cup milk or soymilk
2 Tbsp. oil

Mix together until dry ingredients are moistened. Pour over the top of the corn and tofu mixture in the pan. Bake at 350° F. about 25 minutes until cornbread is golden.

Per Serving: Calories: 331, Protein: 9 gm., Fat: 18 gm., Carbohydrates: 38 gm.

Stuffed Bell Peppers Con Chili

Serves 6

Cut into 1" x 1/2" x 1/4" pieces:
  1 lb. firm tofu

Whip together:
  6 Tbsp. soy sauce
  3 Tbsp. peanut butter
  2 tsp. onion powder
  1/2 tsp. garlic powder

Pour over the tofu in a glass or stainless steel bowl. Mix together and let marinate for 1/2 hour.

Brown in:
  2 Tbsp. oil

Wash and cut off the tops of:
  6 large bell peppers

Remove stems, membranes and seeds, saving the tops. Parboil the shells in 1" boiling water for 5 minutes and set them up in an oiled baking dish.

Saute:
  1/4 cup oil
  1 large onion, chopped
  2 stalks celery, chopped
  6 bell pepper tops, chopped

Add and mix together:
  1 Tbsp. chili powder (more if you like)
  2 cloves garlic, minced
  1/2 tsp. oregano
  1 tsp. cumin
  1 tsp. salt
  1 cup tomato sauce
  1 1/2 cups cut corn
  the browned tofu

Stuff the peppers, pour 1 cup tomato sauce over all and bake at 400° F. for 25 minutes.

Variation: Cut the pepper in half lengthwise before parboiling and stuffing, and bake in a larger pan.

Per Serving: Calories: 308, Protein: 12 gm., Fat: 19 gm., Carbohydrates: 28 gm.

Stuffed Bell Peppers

Serves 6

Have ready:
1 1/2 cups cooked rice, brown or white

Wash, cut off tops and take out seeds and membrane from:
6 large bell peppers

Tomato Sauce

Mix together:

4 cups tomato sauce or 2 (15 oz.) cans   **1/8 tsp. black pepper**
2 tsp. oregano   **1 Tbsp. sugar**
1 tsp. basil   **1 bay leaf**

In another pan, saute:

2 Tbsp. oil   **6 bell pepper tops, stemmed and chopped**
1 small onion, diced   **1 lb. tofu, cut in 1/2" chunks**
2 cloves garlic, pressed

When all this is slightly browned, add it to the sauce, turn heat to low and simmer. Steam the pepper shells in 1/2" water for 5 minutes. Mix 2 1/2 cups sauce with 1 1/2 cups cooked rice. Fill each partially cooked pepper with this and carefully place each one upright in a 9" baking dish. Top with the remaining sauce. Bake at 350° F. for about 30 minutes. Serve hot.

Per Serving: Calories: 244, Protein: 11 gm., Fat: 8 gm., Carbohydrates: 38 gm.

Scalloped Cabbage

Serves 4-6

Parboil for 5 minutes:
1 qt. cabbage, coarsely chopped
1 cup water

Saute:
2 Tbsp. oil
1 onion, chopped

Sprinkle over onion:
2 Tbsp. unbleached white flour
1/2 tsp. salt

Drain cabbage cooking water into onion and flour. Saute mixture and stir over low heat until thick.

Preheat oven to 350° F.

Blend or beat until smooth:

1/2 lb. tofu   **2 Tbsp. vinegar**
1 tsp. salt   **1/8 tsp. black pepper**
2 Tbsp. oil

Stir this mixture into the cabbage along with the sauteed onions. Pour all into 1 1/2-pint baking dish, top with bread crumbs and sprinkle with paprika. Bake for 30 minutes.

Per Serving: Calories: 197, Protein: 6 gm., Fat: 13 gm., Carbohydrates: 12 gm.

Breads

Yeasted Bread and Rolls, Cinnamon Rolls, Flour Tortillas, Sesame Tofu Crackers, and Hush Puppies

BREADS

Pumpernickel Bread

Makes 2 loaves

This is a dark, moist bread.

Dissolve together and let rise until foamy (about 10 minutes):
  3/4 cup warm water
  2 Tbsp. active dry yeast
  2 Tbsp. molasses

Blend in a blender until smooth and creamy:
  1/2 lb. tofu
  3/4 cup warm water

Stir the blended mixture into the foamy yeast mixture along with:
  6 Tbsp. molasses
  1/4 cup oil

Stir in:
  3 cups dark rye flour
  3 cups whole wheat flour
  1 cup bread flour (high gluten)
  2 Tbsp. cocoa powder

Turn the dough out on a floured board and knead until smooth. Place the kneaded dough in an oiled bowl, cover and let rise about 2 hours in a warm place until about double in bulk. Punch down, knead and shape into 2 round or oblong loaves. Let rise until almost double. Bake at 450° F. for 20 minutes. Reduce heat to 350° F. and bake about 30 minutes more or until the loaves sound hollow when tapped on the bottom. Brush oil on the top and let cool on a wire rack.

Per Slice (18 Slices Per Loaf): Calories: 220, Protein: 6 gm., Fat: 6 gm., Carbohydrates: 37 gm.

Yeasted Bread or Rolls
Makes 2 loaves or 36 rolls

Boil until soft:
3 medium potatoes

Set aside.

Dissolve together in a large mixing bowl:
1 cup warm potato water
2 Tbsp. active dry yeast
1 Tbsp. honey

Let rise 10 minutes.

Blend in a blender until smooth and creamy:
1/2 lb. tofu
1 1/2 cups cooked potatoes, mashed and cooled
1 cup warm water

Stir contents of the blender into the foaming yeast mixture.

Stir in:
4 cups unbleached white flour
1 Tbsp. salt
1/2 cup oil

Beat well. Let rise in a warm place for 20 minutes.

Stir down and add:
3-4 cups unbleached white flour

Knead into a smooth, soft dough. Form into 2 loaves or about 36 rolls. Put in oiled pans or oiled cookie sheets. Let rise about 20 minutes, until almost double in bulk. Preheat oven to 375° F. Bake for 40 minutes for loaves or 20 minutes for rolls.

Variation: For Cinnamon Rolls knead the dough into a smooth ball. Divide in half and roll out each half on a well-floured board into a large rectangle 3/16" to 1/4" thick. Sprinkle and spread half of the filling, below, over all of the dough. Roll up each rectangle of dough, jelly-roll style. Slice into 1" rounds and place about 1" apart on oiled cookie sheets. Sprinkle the rest of the filling on top of the rolls. Let rise about 10 minutes. Bake for about 20 minutes.

Cinnamon Roll Filling

Mix together in a bowl:
1 cup unbleached white flour   **1 tsp. salt**
1 cup sugar   **1/2 cup oil**
1 Tbsp. cinnamon

Stir in:
1/2 cup raisins

Per Slice (18 Slices Per Loaf): Calories: 138, Protein: 3 gm., Fat: 4 gm., Carbohydrates: 21 gm.

Per Cinnamon Roll: Calories: 206, Protein: 4 gm., Fat: 7 gm., Carbohydrates: 31 gm.

Danish

Makes 18 danish

Dough

Dissolve together:
1 (1 Tbsp.) pkg. active dry yeast   **1 cup warm water**

Let stand 5 minutes, then mix in:
2 cups unbleached white flour   **1/4 cup sugar or honey**

Beat well and let rise until doubled.

Dissolve together, then mix into the flour and yeast mixture with your hands:
1/2 cup oil   **1 tsp. salt**
1/4 cup sugar

Add to make a kneadable dough:
about 1 1/2 cups more unbleached white flour

Knead until smooth and soft, but not sticky. Let rise until double again.

Tofu Filling

Blend in a blender until smooth and creamy:
1/2 cup water   **1 cup soft tofu, crumbled**
1/2 cup oil

Pour this into a bowl and whisk in:
1/4 cup fresh lemon juice   **1/2 tsp. salt**
1/2 cup sugar or honey   **2 Tbsp. unbleached white flour**

Whisk all together. Cook over medium heat, stirring constantly until thickened. Remove from heat and cool before filling the danish dough. Preheat oven to 350° F. Roll the dough out to 1/8" thick. Brush with oil and cut into 3" x 3" squares. Place 1-2 tablespoons of filling in the center of each square. You can add about 1 tablespoon of cherry or blueberry pie filling on top of the Tofu Filling. Fold two opposite corners of the dough toward the middle and pinch together. Take the remaining unfolded corners and curl them in toward the filling. Let rise 5 minutes. Place on a well-oiled cookie sheet. Leave 1/2" to 1" space between each danish. Bake for about 15 minutes or until light golden brown. Brush with oil for last 3 minutes of baking.

Variation: For Prune Danish, place 1-2 tablespoons Prune Filling, below, instead of Tofu Filling, in the center of each square. Bring all four corners toward the middle and pinch together. Place on a well-oiled cookie sheet and follow the baking instructions, above.

Prune Filling

Cook covered until tender and then put through a food mill to make puree:
1 (16 oz.) box prunes, pitted   **2 cups water**

Stir in:
1 1/2 Tbsp. fresh lemon juice

Per Danish (With Tofu Filling): Calories: 287, Protein: 4 gm., Fat: 13 gm., Carbohydrates: 39 gm.

Per Danish (With Prune Filling): Calories: 211, Protein: 3 gm., Fat: 6 gm., Carbohydrates: 35 gm.

Danish

Rum Rolls

Filled rolls for breakfast or brunch.

Preheat oven to 400° F.

Dissolve together:
  1/2 cup warm water
  1 Tbsp. active dry yeast
  1/2 cup sugar

Let foam together in a warm place 5-10 minutes. Then mix in:
  1 cup unbleached white flour

Let sit 5-10 minutes more. Then mix in:
  1/2 cup oil
  4-5 cups more unbleached white flour
  1 tsp. salt

Stir until well blended. Cover and let rise in a warm place until double. While dough is rising, prepare filling below. Punch dough down and divide in half. Roll each half into a rectangle 3/8″ thick. Spread with filling, below, roll up each rectangle and cut into 1″ thick slices. Put each slice into an oiled muffin cup. Cover and let rise until almost double. Bake for 15-20 minutes. Cool and brush with frosting, below. These rolls also freeze well.

Filling

Beat together:
  1 cup brown sugar
  1/2 lb. tofu, crumbled
  2 Tbsp. oil
  2 tsp. rum flavoring
  1/2 tsp. salt

Stir in:
  1 cup raisins, plumped in hot water and drained

Frosting

Beat together and brush over the rolls:
  1 cup powdered sugar
  2-3 Tbsp. hot water
  1 tsp. rum flavoring

Per Roll: Calories: 257, Protein: 4 gm., Fat: 7 gm., Carbohydrates: 44 gm.

English Muffins

Mix in a large bowl and let sit 10 minutes:
1 pkg. (1 Tbsp.) active dry yeast
1 cup warm water
2 Tbsp. sugar

Blend in a blender until smooth and creamy:
1/2 lb. tofu
1/2 cup warm water
1 tsp. salt

Pour this into the foaming yeast mixture along with:
3 Tbsp. oil

Stir in until smooth:
3 1/2 cups unbleached white flour

Mix in to make a soft dough:
1-1 1/2 cups unbleached white flour

Knead on a floured board for about 5 minutes. Let the dough rise in an oiled bowl until almost double in bulk. Punch down the dough and divide in half. Roll each half out on a generous amount of cornmeal to 1/2" thick. Cut dough in 3" circles. Let rise 10 minutes. Cook on a dry griddle or cast iron skillet over low heat for about 5-8 minutes on each side or until golden brown.

Per Muffin: Calories: 168, Protein: 5 gm., Fat: 3 gm., Carbohydrates: 28 gm.

Flour Tortillas

Mix together in a medium mixing bowl:
4 cups unbleached white flour
1 tsp. salt

Stir in:
1/3 cup oil

Blend in a blender until smooth:
1/2 lb. soft tofu
1 1/4 cups water

Make a well in the flour mixture, add liquid and stir well. Knead into a smooth dough on a well-floured board. Divide into 14-16 balls about 1 1/2" in diameter. On a floured board roll each ball out into an 8" circle .

Cook on a hot, dry griddle for a few seconds on each side until bubbly and brown-flecked on each side. Tortillas are best served right off the griddle, but can also be stacked inside a damp towel and reheated later.

Per Tortilla: Calories: 190, Protein: 5 gm., Fat: 6 gm., Carbohydrates: 27 gm.

Tofu Biscuits

These are filling, high-protein biscuits.

Preheat oven to 425° F.

Mix together in a medium bowl:
2 cups unbleached white flour
2 tsp. baking powder
1/2 tsp. salt

Cut in:
1/4 cup oil

Blend in a blender until smooth:
1/2 cup water
1/2 cup soft tofu

Make a hole in the center of the flour mixture and pour in blended liquid. Stir well. Roll out dough on floured board, handling as little as possible. Cut with biscuit cutter or sharp knife. Bake for 15 minutes.

Per Biscuit: Calories: 130, Protein: 3 gm., Fat: 5 gm., Carbohydrates: 17 gm.

Tofu French Toast

A breakfast treat.

Blend in a blender until smooth and creamy:
1 1/2 cups tofu
1 1/2 tsp. cinnamon
1/4 cup honey
1 tsp. salt
1/2 cup water
2 Tbsp. oil

Pour into a shallow bowl.

Dip slices of day-old whole grain or home-made bread in batter, then fry in a hot skillet with 1 tablespoon oil for each side. Brown well on both sides. Serve with honey or maple syrup.

Per Slice: Calories: 243, Protein: 10 gm., Fat: 15 gm., Carbohydrates: 11 gm.

Buckwheat Cakes

Mix together well in a large mixing bowl:

1 cup unbleached white flour
1 cup buckwheat flour
1/4 cup oatmeal
1/4 cup sugar

2 tsp. baking powder
1 tsp. baking soda
1 1/4 tsp. salt

Blend in a blender until smooth and creamy:

1/2 lb. soft tofu
3 cups water
1/3 cup oil

Make a well in the dry ingredients and pour in the wet ones. Stir until the batter is smooth. It will look gooey.

Heat the griddle over medium-high heat. Oil lightly and pour 1/4 cup batter for each cake. When the tops of the cakes bubble and look dry, flip them over and brown the other side. Serve hot with honey, syrup or jam.

Per Pancake: Calories: 113, Protein: 3 gm., Fat: 6 gm., Carbohydrates: 13 gm.

Tofu Pancakes

Mix thoroughly together:

2 cups unbleached white flour
1/2 cup cornmeal
4 1/2 tsp. baking powder

1 tsp. salt
1/4 cup sugar (or add 1/4 cup honey
  to wet ingredients)

Gently stir in with only a few strokes:

3 cups milk or soymilk
2 Tbsp. oil

Batter will be lumpy.

Fold in gently:

1/2 lb. tofu, drained and well crumbled

Let batter sit while griddle heats. Fry on a lightly oiled griddle and serve.

Per Pancake: Calories: 78, Protein: 3 gm., Fat: 4 gm., Carbohydrates: 11 gm.

Banana Bread

Preheat oven to 350° F.

Blend in a blender until smooth and creamy:
3/4 cup tofu

Pour into a mixing bowl and beat in:
1 cup sugar   **1 tsp. vanilla**
1/4 cup oil   **1 cup ripe bananas, mashed**

Mix together in another bowl:
2 cups unbleached white flour   **1/2 tsp. baking soda**
1/2 tsp. baking powder   **1/4 tsp. salt**

Beat everything together, then fold in:
3/4 cup walnut pieces

Pour into an oiled loaf pan. Bake for about 1 hour.

Per Slice (12 Slices Per Loaf): Calories: 262, Protein: 5 gm., Fat: 10 gm., Carbohydrates: 39 gm.

Hush Puppies

Mix together in a 3 quart bowl:
2 cups unbleached white flour   **1 1/4 tsp. salt**
2 cups cornmeal   **4 tsp. baking powder**

Blend in a blender until smooth:
1/2 lb. soft tofu
1 1/2 cups water

Stir in:
1/4 cup oil

Make a well in the middle of the dry ingredients and add liquid. Stir until all ingredients are moistened.

Add:
1/2 cup onion, finely chopped

Mix all together. Use 2 tablespoons dough to form a log or ball and fry them in 1" oil at 350° F. Brown on both sides. Serve as they are or with mustard.

Variation: for Sweet Hush Puppies, omit the onion and add 2 tablespoons honey or sugar to liquid ingredients. Serve hot with honey or jam.

Per Pup: Calories: 126, Protein: 3 gm., Fat: 5 gm., Carbohydrates: 16 gm.

Cornmeal Muffins

Makes 12 muffins

Preheat oven to 425° F.

Mix together:
2 cups cornmeal
2 cups unbleached white flour
1 1/2 tsp. salt
2 tsp. baking powder
1/2 tsp. baking soda

Blend in a blender until smooth and creamy:
1/2 lb. soft tofu
1 1/2 cups water

Pour into bowl and then stir in:
1/4 cup oil
3 Tbsp. honey or molasses

Stir the wet ingredients into the dry ingredients until moistened. Fill oiled muffin tins three-quarters full. Bake for 15-20 minutes or until golden brown.

Per Muffin: Calories: 232, Protein: 6 gm., Fat: 7 gm., Carbohydrates: 36 gm.

Sesame Tofu Crackers

Makes 50 crackers

Preheat oven to 400° F.

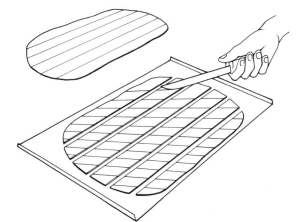

Mix together in a bowl:
3 cups unbleached white flour or
  whole wheat flour
1 tsp. salt
3 Tbsp. sesame seeds
1 tsp. baking powder

In a blender, blend until smooth and creamy:
1/2 lb. tofu
1/2 cup oil
1/4 cup water

Make a well in the middle of the dry ingredients and pour in the blended mix. Mix well. Add up to 1/4 cup water if necessary to make a soft dough.

Roll out on a lightly floured board to 1/16" thick and cut in 3" x 14" strips. Place on a cookie sheet and cut the strips diagonally.

Bake for 12-15 minutes or until golden brown. Watch them carefully so they don't burn. These will keep well if stored in an airtight container.

Per Cracker: Calories: 55, Protein: 1 gm., Fat: 3 gm., Carbohydrates: 6 gm.

Noodles

Blend in a blender until smooth and creamy:
1/2 lb. tofu
2 Tbsp. oil
1/2 tsp. salt

Pour this into:
1 3/4 cups unbleached white flour

Mix and knead until smooth and soft (about 10 minutes). Put through a noodle machine or roll out by hand and cut. Let dry 15 minutes. Boil in salted water about 5 minutes.

Per Serving: Calories: 254, Protein: 8 gm., Fat: 7 gm., Carbohydrates: 36 gm.

Spinach Noodles

Blend in a blender until smooth and creamy:
1 cup fresh spinach, washed, dried and chopped
1/2 cup tofu
2 Tbsp. oil
1/2 tsp. salt

Pour this into:
2 cups unbleached white flour

Mix and knead until smooth and soft (about 10 minutes). Put through a noodle machine or roll out by hand and cut. Let dry 15 minutes. Boil in salted water about 5 minutes.

Per Serving: Calories: 265, Protein: 8 gm., Fat: 7 gm., Carbohydrates: 40 gm.

Noodles and Spinach Noodles

Cookies and Bars

Clockwise starting from Soymilk: Oatmeal, Peanut Butter and Soft Molasses Cookies, Jam Dot Cookies, Chocolate Brownies, Chocolate Chip Bars, Date-Nut Bars, and Carob Honey Brownies

COOKIES AND BARS

Jam Dot Cookies

Makes 48 cookies

Preheat oven to 350° F.

Have ready:
1/4 cup any flavor of jam

Blend in a blender until creamy:
1/2 lb. tofu
1/2 cup walnuts

Pour the blended mixture into a bowl and mix in:

1/2 cup oil	**1 tsp. salt**
2 cups sugar	**1 tsp. baking soda**
1 tsp. vanilla	**4 cups unbleached white flour**

Mix well by hand or electric mixer. Roll into 1 1/2" balls and place them 2" apart on oiled cookie sheets. Press thumb in the middle of each ball, leaving a depression. Bake for 10 minutes, remove sheets from oven and drop 1/4 teaspoon of jam in each depression. Bake 2-3 minutes more. Store when cool with wax paper between layers.

Per Cookie: Calories: 110, Protein: 2 gm., Fat: 3 gm., Carbohydrates: 17 gm.

Carob Honey Brownies

Makes one 9" square pan

Preheat oven to 350° F.

Blend in a blender until creamy:

1/2 lb. soft tofu	**1 Tbsp. vanilla**
1 cup honey	**2/3 cup carob powder**
1/2 cup oil	**3/4 cup water**

In a separate bowl, mix:
1 3/4 cups unbleached flour
3/4 tsp. baking soda
1 tsp. baking powder

Add wet ingredients and mix well.

Fold in:
1/2 cup walnuts, chopped

Oil and flour a 9" square pan. Spread batter evenly. Bake for 25-30 minutes. Cool and cut into 12 brownies.

Per Brownie: Calories: 293, Protein: 4 gm., Fat: 13 gm., Carbohydrates: 47 gm.

Brownies

Preheat oven to 350° F.

Whisk together in a saucepan, leaving no lumps:
1/3 cup unbleached white flour
2/3 cup water

Whip in:
1/2 lb. tofu, blended until smooth and creamy

Stir constantly over low heat until thickened. Cool completely.

To the cooled mixture, add:
2 cups sugar
1 tsp. salt
1 tsp. vanilla

Beat well.

In another bowl mix together:
3/4 cup cocoa powder
1/2 cup oil

Add to the other ingredients and stir well.

Mix together:
1 1/2 cups unbleached white flour
1 scant tsp. baking powder

Add this to the mixture above and stir until there are no lumps. Bake in a well-oiled and floured 10" square pan for 25 minutes or until a knife inserted in the middle comes out clean. Cut into 12 brownies.

For cake-like brownies, increase baking powder to 2 teaspoons and bake for 20 minutes.

Per Brownie: Calories: 383, Protein: 6 gm., Fat: 12 gm., Carbohydrates: 64 gm.

Soft Molasses Cookies

Preheat oven to 350° F.

Blend in a blender until smooth and creamy:
1 cup molasses or sorghum   **1/2 lb. tofu, mashed**
1 cup oil   **1/2 cup brown sugar**

Mix together dry ingredients:
3 1/2-4 cups unbleached white flour
1/2 tsp. baking soda
1/4 tsp. salt

Mix together wet and dry ingredients until well blended. Drop by spoonfuls onto an oiled cookie sheet. Bake for about 10 minutes. Store in tightly covered container to preserve moisture.

Per Cookie: Calories: 144, Protein: 2 gm., Fat: 7 gm., Carbohydrates: 9 gm.

Oatmeal Cookies

Makes 48 cookies

Preheat oven to 350° F.

Blend in a blender until smooth and creamy:
3/4 cup soft tofu

Pour into a bowl and mix together with:
1 cup oil
1 1/2 cups honey
1 Tbsp. vanilla

In another bowl mix together:
4 cups rolled oats   **1 tsp. baking soda**
2 1/2 cups unbleached white flour   **1/2 tsp. salt**
1 tsp. baking powder

Mix the dry ingredients into the wet along with:
1/2 cup walnuts, broken
1/2 cup raisins

Drop by heaping tablespoonfuls onto oiled cookie sheets and bake for 15 minutes.

Per Cookie: Calories: 121, Protein: 2 gm., Fat: 4 gm., Carbohydrates: 20 gm.

Gingerbread Cut-Out Cookies

Makes 18 large cookies

Preheat oven to 350° F.

Blend in a blender until smooth and creamy:
1/2 lb. tofu   **1 cup molasses**
1/2 cup oil   **1 cup brown sugar**

Pour this mixture into a large mixing bowl.

In another bowl mix together dry ingredients:
7 cups unbleached white flour   **1/2 tsp. allspice**
2 tsp. baking soda   **1/4 tsp. cloves**
4 tsp. ginger   **1/4 tsp. nutmeg**
2 tsp. cinnamon   **1 tsp. salt**

Add half of the mixed dry ingredients to the wet ones and stir until smooth, then add the rest of the dry ingredients. The dough can be mixed either by hand or electric mixer. If you are mixing with a spoon, you may actually have to use your hands to mix the last part. Chill the dough overnight, then roll out 1/8″ to 1/4″ thick. Cut in desired shapes and bake on oiled cookie sheets for about 8 minutes.

Per Cookie: Calories: 349, Protein: 6 gm., Fat: 7 gm., Carbohydrates: 63 gm.

Peanut Butter Cookies

Makes 48 cookies

Preheat oven to 350° F.

Mix together:
3 cup unbleached white flour
1 tsp. baking soda
1/2 tsp. salt

In another bowl mix together:

1/2 cup oil	**1/2 cup honey**
1 cup peanut butter	**1/2 cup tofu, blended**
1 cup brown sugar	**1 tsp. vanilla**

Mix the dry ingredients into the wet ones. Form the dough into 1" balls. Arrange the balls on a cookie sheet about 3" apart. Press with a fork (that has been dipped in cold water) in a crisscross design, then bake for 10-12 minutes.

Per Cookie: Calories: 112, Protein: 2 gm., Fat: 5 gm., Carbohydrates: 12 gm.

Tofu Fudge Chews

Makes 48 cookies

These cookies keep well in an airtight container. They have a moist, chewy center with a crisp, sugar-coated outside.

Blend in a blender until smooth:
1/2 lb. tofu
1/2 cup oil

Pour into a medium mixing bowl. Add:

1 1/2 cups sugar	**1 Tbsp. vanilla (optional)**
1/2 cup cocoa powder	**1 Tbsp. water, milk or soymilk**

Stir well. Mix separately:
3 cups unbleached white flour
1 tsp. baking soda
1 tsp. salt

Add to wet ingredients. Mix well. The dough should be fairly stiff. Roll into 1 1/2" balls. In a saucer put:
1/2 cup sugar

Roll the formed balls in the sugar until they are coated. Place on a lightly oiled cookie sheet 1" apart. Bake for 12-15 minutes at 350° F. Cool on a wire rack.

Per Cookie: Calories: 92, Protein: 1 gm., Fat: 3 gm., Carbohydrates: 15 gm.

Date-Nut Bars

Makes one 9" x 13" pan

Preheat oven to 375° F.

Cook over low heat until thickened:
2 (8 oz.) pkgs. (2 1/2 cups) dates, pitted and chopped
2 1/2 cups water

Set aside while preparing the following cookie mix.

Beat together in a medium mixing bowl:
1/2 cup tofu, soft and mashed   **3/4 cup honey**
1/2 cup oil   **1 tsp. salt**

Add and beat in:
2 cups unbleached white flour   **1 cup nuts, chopped**
1 1/2 cups oats, quick-cooking   **(almonds, pecans, walnuts or peanuts)**
3/4 tsp. baking soda

Press three-quarters of the dough into an oiled 9" x 13" pan. Spread date filling evenly over dough. Crumble remaining dough over dates. Bake for 15-20 minutes. Cool and cut into 24 bars.

Note: For a crunchier cookie, substitute 3/4 cup brown sugar for the honey.

Per Bar: Calories: 487, Protein: 6 gm., Fat: 8 gm., Carbohydrates: 105 gm.

Jam Bars

Makes one 9" x 13" pan

Preheat oven to 375° F.

Blend in a blender until smooth and creamy:
1 lb. tofu   **2 Tbsp. sugar**
6 Tbsp. oil   **1/2 tsp. salt**
7 Tbsp. fresh lemon juice

Mix in a bowl:
1 1/2 cups sugar   **1/4 cup oil**
1/2 cup brown sugar, packed   **1 1/2 cups of the blended mixture above**
1 1/2 tsp. vanilla

Add and mix in well:
4 cups unbleached white flour   **1/4 tsp. cinnamon**
1 tsp. baking soda

Press three-quarters of this dough into an oiled and floured 9" x 13" pan. Bake for 10 minutes. Take it out of the oven and spread with:
1/2 cup jam

On top of the jam spread the rest of the blended tofu mixture (about 1/2 cup).

Add to the remaining dough:
1/2 cup flour

Mix well and crumble on top. Bake 10 minutes more. Cut into 24 bars and serve.

Per Bar: Calories: 252, Protein: 4 gm., Fat: 7 gm., Carbohydrates: 37 gm.

Pecan-Coconut Bars

Makes one 9" square pan

Preheat oven to 350° F.

Beat with an electric beater:

1/2 cup tofu, mashed	**2 Tbsp. lemon juice**
1/3 cup oil	**1 tsp. salt**

Beat in:

1 cup brown sugar, packed	**2/3 cup dried coconut**
1 1/2 cups unbleached white flour	**1 tsp. vanilla**
1/2 cup oatmeal	**1 tsp. baking powder**

Fold in:
1/2 cup pecan pieces

Pour into an oiled pan. Bake for 25-30 minutes. Cool, and cut into 12 bars.

Per Bar: Calories: 268, Protein: 4 gm., Fat: 13 gm., Carbohydrates: 34 gm.

Chocolate Chip Bars

Makes one 9" x 13" pan

Preheat oven to 350° F.

Cream together:
3/4 cup white sugar
3/4 cup brown sugar
1 cup oil

Blend in a blender:
1/3 cup tofu, mashed
2 Tbsp. water
1 tsp. vanilla

Add to the sugar and oil. In a bowl mix together:

3 1/2 cups unbleached white flour	**1/2 tsp. baking soda**
1 1/2 tsp. baking powder	**1/2 tsp. salt**

Mix wet and dry ingredients together, then fold in:
1 cup chocolate chips

Press into a 9" x 13" pan and bake 10-12 minutes, until lightly browned. Cool and cut into 24 bars.

Per Bar: Calories: 229, Protein: 3 gm., Fat: 10 gm., Carbohydrates: 33 gm.

Desserts

Clockwise from top left: Cheesecake, Gingerbread Cut-Out Cookies, Carrot Cake, Pumpkin Pie, Creamy Coconut Pie, Black Bottom Pie, and Gingerbread Cut-Out Cookies
Center: Strawberry Pudding and Apricot Whip

DESSERTS

Orange-Vanilla "Custard"

Serves 8-10
Makes one 9 1/2" deep-dish pie pan

Be sure to read "Blending Tofu," on p. 7., before blending more than 1/2 lb. at a time.

Preheat oven to 400° F.

Blend in a blender until smooth and creamy:
   2 lbs. tofu, crumbled
   2/3 cup frozen orange juice concentrate, thawed
   1/4 cup oil
   1 tsp. vanilla
   1/2 tsp. salt

In a bowl, mix:
   1 cup sugar
   1/2 cup flour
   1 tsp. baking powder
   1/4 tsp. baking soda

Add this mixture slowly to the mixture in the blender, blending until smooth.

Pour the mixture into the well-oiled and floured pan. Bake for about 30 minutes. Serve hot or cold. Slice with a sharp wet knife. The texture becomes denser as it cools.

Per Serving: Calories: 293, Protein: 9 gm., Fat: 12 gm., Carbohydrates: 40 gm.

Banana Dessert

Serves 4-6

Quick and easy.

Preheat oven to 350° F.

Blend in a blender until smooth and creamy:
   1 lb. tofu, mashed
   1/2 tsp. salt
   1/4 cup oil
   3 Tbsp. vinegar or lemon juice
   1 1/4 cups sugar
   1 1/2-2 tsp. cinnamon

Set aside. Cut 6 firm bananas or an equal amount of plantanos in half lengthwise. Fry the banana halves in oil over medium heat until golden brown. Arrange half of the bananas flat side up and cover with half the blended tofu mixture. Arrange the rest of the bananas on top and cover with the rest of the blended tofu mixture. Bake for 20-30 minutes. Serve hot.

Per Serving: Calories: 510, Protein: 9 gm., Fat: 21 gm., Carbohydrates: 81 gm.

Plum Noodle Kugel

Preheat oven to 350° F.

Mix together:

1 lb. flat noodles, cooked and drained
1 1/2 cups sugar
1 1/2 lbs. tofu, mashed

1 1/2 cups applesauce
1 1/2 tsp. cinnamon
3 lbs. plums (canned) pitted and quartered

Spread this mixture evenly in an oiled 9" x 13" pan.

Mix together:

3/4 cup chopped nuts
3/4 cup fine whole grain bread crumbs

Crumble this mixture evenly over the top, then drizzle with:

3 Tbsp. oil

Bake for 45 minutes. Serve hot or cold with Sweet and Creamy Topping, p. 145.

Per Serving: Calories: 425, Protein: 11 gm., Fat: 11 gm., Carbohydrates: 71 gm.

Pumpkin Pie

A holiday favorite.

Preheat oven to 350° F.

Have ready:

1 unbaked 9" pastry crust

Blend in a blender until smooth and creamy:

3/4 lb. tofu
1 (16 oz.) can pumpkin (2 cups)
1 1/2 tsp. cinnamon
3/4 tsp. ginger
1/2 tsp. nutmeg
1 tsp. salt
1/3 cup oil
1 tsp. vanilla
1 cup light brown sugar
1 1/2 Tbsp. molasses

Pour this mixture into unbaked pastry shell. Bake for 1 hour. Chill and serve with Sweet and Creamy Topping, p. 145.

Per Serving: Calories: 405, Protein: 6 gm., Fat: 21 gm., Carbohydrates: 40 gm.

Creamy Coconut Pie

Serves 6-8
Makes one 9" pie

Quick and easy.

Preheat oven to 350° F.

Have ready:
1 prebaked graham cracker pie shell

Blend in a blender until smooth and creamy:
1 1/2 lbs. tofu
1/2 cup oil
2 tsp. vanilla
1/2 tsp. salt
1 1/2 cups powdered sugar

Fold in:
2 cups coconut, dried and sweetened

Pour into the pie shell. Bake for 15 minutes.

Sprinkle on top:
1/4 cup coconut

Bake another 5 minutes or until the filling looks firm and set. Serve chilled.

Per Serving: Calories: 610, Protein: 11 gm., Fat: 42 gm., Carbohydrates: 45 gm.

Black Bottom Pie

Serves 6
Makes one 8" pie

Have ready:
1 1/2 cups Sweet and Creamy Topping, p. 145, chilled
one 8" baked graham cracker crust or pastry shell, cooled

Blend in a blender until smooth and creamy:
1 lb. tofu
1 1/2 cups confectioner's sugar
3/4 cup oil
6 Tbsp. cocoa
1 Tbsp. vanilla
3/4 tsp. soy sauce

Cover the bottom of a thoroughly cooled graham cracker pie crust with:
1/2 oz. unsweetened baking chocolate, grated or shaved

Then pour in the pudding. Chill overnight. Top with Sweet and Creamy Topping, p. 145, and garnish with unsweetened chocolate shavings.

Per Serving: Calories: 608, Protein: 8 gm., Fat: 46 gm., Carbohydrates: 50 gm.

Frozen Peanut Butter Pie

Serves 6-8
Makes one 9" pie

A deliciously creamy, frozen dessert that is very easy to make.

Have ready:
one 9" baked pie shell

Blend in a blender until smooth and creamy:
1 lb. tofu	**1/4 cup oil**
3/4 cup peanut butter	**1 tsp. vanilla**
1/2 cup honey	**1/8 tsp. salt**

Pour into the baked pie shell. Decorate with semi-sweet chocolate shavings or curls. Freeze. Before serving let thaw for about 10 minutes.

Per Serving: Calories: 529, Protein: 16 gm., Fat: 29 gm., Carbohydrates: 55 gm.

Cannoli

Makes 6-7

A melt-in-your-mouth Sicilian pastry.

Have ready:
cannoli molds or a piece of 1" x 6" wooden dowel
(a clean piece of broomstick would work)

Cannoli Shell Dough

Combine:
1 cup unbleached white flour	**1/2 tsp. cinnamon (optional)**
1 Tbsp. sugar	**1/4 tsp. salt**

Stir in to form a ball:
9 Tbsp. water

Form the dough into 6-7 balls. Roll each one out on a lightly floured board until 5 to 6 inches in diameter (or you can roll the dough out whole and cut into 5" squares). Place a mold or dowel in the center of a circle or square of dough, fold around the mold and seal lengthwise edges with a dab of water. Deep-fry in oil at 350° F. until light brown (about 2 minutes) and drain on absorbent paper. Remove the mold or dowel and start the next shell. Be careful not to let the oil smoke. Let all the shells cool before filling.

Cannoli Filling

Blend in a blender until smooth and creamy:
1/2 lb. tofu	**1 cup confectioners sugar**
5 Tbsp. oil	**1/2 tsp. almond extract**
3 Tbsp. lemon juice	

Pour into a bowl and fold in:
2 Tbsp. citron, finely diced	**2 Tbsp. chocolate chips**

Chill the filling before stuffing the shells and serve immediately.

Per Serving: Calories: 347, Protein: 5 gm., Fat: 19 gm., Carbohydrates: 41 gm.

TOFU CHEESECAKES

Tofu Cheesecakes can be made in a variety of flavors and sweeteners. A medium firm tofu is good for cheesecake. Be sure to read "Blending Tofu" on p. 7. If your tofu is very soft, it is best to put it between two towels, then put a weight on it for a while. When a Tofu Cheesecake is done baking, it will be slightly risen on the edges with small cracks appearing on the surface. The middle will not have risen, but will be springy to slight pressure from a finger. It will have a dry firm look.

Cheesecake

Serves 6-8
Makes one 10" pie or 10" spring form pan

Quick and easy.

Preheat oven to 375° F.

Have ready:
1 baked graham cracker pie shell

Blend in a blender until smooth and creamy:
2 lbs. tofu
3 Tbsp. lemon juice
1 Tbsp. vanilla
1/2 tsp. salt

1/2 cup oil
1/2 cup honey
1 cup sugar

Pour this mixture into the baked crust. Bake for 40 minutes. Serve well chilled topped with fresh or frozen fruit.

Per Serving: Calories: 552, Protein: 12 gm., Fat: 30 gm., Carbohydrates: 51 gm.

Honey Cheesecake

Serves 6-8
Makes one 9" pie

Quick and easy.

Preheat oven to 350° F.

Have ready:
1 baked 9" graham cracker pie shell

Blend in a blender until smooth and creamy:
2 lbs. tofu
1/2 cup oil
1 cup honey

3 1/2 Tbsp. lemon juice
1/2 tsp. salt
1 Tbsp. vanilla

Pour this mixture into the baked pie shell and bake for 1 hour.

Serve well-chilled topped with fresh or frozen fruit.

Per Serving: Calories: 517, Protein: 11 gm., Fat: 33 gm., Carbohydrates: 54 gm.

Chocolate Cheesecake and Honey Cheesecake

Chocolate Cheesecake

Serves 10-12
Makes one 10" spring form pan

This recipe is pictured on p. 138.

Have ready in the bottom of a 10" spring form pan:
1 prebaked graham cracker crust

Drain between 2 towels with a breadboard weight on top for about 20 minutes:
2 1/2 lbs. tofu

Blend the drained tofu, 1/2 pound at a time, until smooth and creamy. With each 1/2 pound in the blender add:
1/2 cup sugar (2 1/2 cups in all)

Pour all the blended tofu and sugar into a bowl.

Preheat oven to 350° F.

Melt in a double boiler and add to the blended tofu mixture:
6 (1 oz.) squares semi-sweet chocolate

Mix together well along with:
2 tsp. vanilla   **pinch of salt**
1 tsp. almond extract   **1/2 cup more sugar**

Pour this mixture into the prebaked crust, then bake for about 40 minutes. When chilled, top with fresh fruit glaze.

Per Serving: Calories: 381, Protein: 9 gm., Fat: 17 gm., Carbohydrates: 58 gm.

Maple Tofu Cheesecake

Serves 4-6
Makes one 8" pie

Quick and easy.

Preheat oven to 350° F.

Blend in a blender until smooth and creamy:
1 1/2 lbs. tofu, mashed   **1 1/3 cups maple syrup**
1/4 cup oil   **pinch of salt**

Pour this mixture into unbaked pie shell. Bake for about 1 hour or until set. Serve cold, topped with maple syrup and pecans or Sweet and Creamy Topping, p. 145.

Per Serving: Calories: 552, Protein: 13 gm., Fat: 22 gm., Carbohydrates: 23 gm.

Lemon Pudding, Chocolate Pudding and Vanilla Pudding

TOFU PUDDINGS

Tofu Puddings are a creamy, delicious, high-protein treat. A medium or Japanese-style tofu is good for making puddings. Read "Blending Tofu" on p. 7 before starting. Puddings can be served chilled in individual serving dishes or chilled in a baked pie shell. For a creamy, frozen dessert, pour any flavor pudding into a baked pie shell and then freeze. Let the pie thaw for 15 minutes before slicing and serving.

For calorie-counters, these puddings can be made without oil (you may need to add some other liquid) and the sweeteners lessened. Banana-Date and Orange-Date Puddings use only the fruit for sweeteners.

Vanilla Pudding

Makes 4 cups

Blend in a blender until smooth and creamy:

1 1/2 lbs. tofu
1/2 cup oil
1 cup sugar or 7/8 cup honey

1 Tbsp. vanilla
1/4 tsp. salt.

Pour into individual serving dishes or baked pie shell. Chill until set and serve.

Per 1/2 Cup Serving: Calories: 278, Protein: 7 gm., Fat: 17 gm., Carbohydrates: 27 gm.

Orange-Date Pudding

Makes 5 cups

This pudding is sweetened by orange juice and dates.

Blend in a blender until smooth and creamy:

1 1/2 lbs. soft tofu	1 tsp. vanilla
3/4 cup pitted dates	1/8 tsp. salt
1/3 cup oil	1/2 cup frozen orange juice concentrate

Pour into individual serving dishes or a baked pie shell. Chill until firm and serve.

Per 1/2 Cup Serving: Calories: 181, Protein: 6 gm., Fat: 10 gm., Carbohydrates: 19 gm.

Orange Pudding

Makes 4 1/2 cups

Blend in a blender until smooth and creamy:

1 1/2 lbs. soft tofu	1 tsp. vanilla
1/4 cup oil	1/8 tsp. salt
3/4 cup sugar	3/4 cup frozen orange juice concentrate

Pour into individual serving dishes or a baked pie shell. Chill until firm and serve.

Per 1/2 Cup Serving: Calories: 212, Protein: 6 gm., Fat: 9 gm., Carbohydrates: 28 gm.

Chocolate Pudding

Makes 4 cups

Blend in a blender until smooth and creamy:

1 1/2 lbs. tofu	1/3 cup cocoa
1/2 cup oil	1/4 tsp. salt or soy sauce
1 1/4 cups sugar	1 1/2 tsp. vanilla

Pour into individual serving dishes or baked pie shell. Chill until firm and serve.

Per 1/2 Cup Serving: Calories: 311, Protein: 7 gm., Fat: 18 gm., Carbohydrates: 35 gm.

Banana Pudding

Makes 3 cups

Blend in a blender until smooth and creamy:

1 lb. tofu	2 tsp. vanilla
1/4 cup oil	2 bananas, ripe
1/4 tsp. salt	1/2 cup sugar

Pour into individual serving dishes or baked pie shell. Chill until set and serve.

Per 1/2 Cup Serving: 240, Protein: 6 gm., Fat: 12 gm., Carbohydrates: 29 gm.

Banana-Date Pudding

Makes 3 cups

This pudding is sweetened by fruit.

Blend in a blender until smooth and creamy:

1 lb. tofu	**1 tsp. lemon juice**
1/4 cup oil	**1/4 tsp. salt**
2 tsp. vanilla	**1/2 cup pitted dates, chopped**
2 Tbsp. milk or soymilk	**2 bananas, ripe**

Pour into individual serving dishes or baked pie shell. Chill until set and serve.

Per 1/2 Cup Serving: Calories: 251, Protein: 7 gm., Fat: 13 gm., Carbohydrates: 32 gm.

Banana Honey Pudding

Makes 4 cups

Blend in a blender until smooth and creamy:

1 1/2 lbs. tofu	**1/2 cup honey**
1/3 cup oil	**1 Tbsp. vanilla**
1/4 tsp. salt	**3 medium bananas, ripe**

Pour into individual serving dishes or baked pie shell. Chill at least 4 hours.

Per 1/2 Cup Serving: Calories: 261, Protein: 8 gm., Fat: 13 gm., Carbohydrates: 32 gm.

Carob Honey Pudding

Makes 3 1/2 cups

Blend in a blender until smooth and creamy:

1 1/2 lbs. tofu	**1 Tbsp. vanilla**
2/3 cup carob powder	**2 tsp. lemon juice**
1/3 cup oil	**1/4 tsp. salt**
1/2 cup honey	

Pour into individual serving dishes or baked pie shell. Chill until firm and serve.

Per 1/2 Cup Serving: Calories: 255, Protein: 8 gm., Fat: 14 gm., Carbohydrates: 32 gm.

Apricot Whip

Makes 3 1/2 cups

Steam over boiling water until soft:
18-20 dried apricot halves (about 1/2 cup)

Blend soft apricots in a blender until smooth and creamy with:

1 lb. tofu	**1/8 tsp. salt**
1/2 cup honey or sugar	**1/4 cup oil**

Pour into individual serving dishes. Chill until set and serve.

Per 1/2 Cup Serving: Calories: 194, Protein: 5 gm., Fat: 11 gm., Carbohydrates: 22 gm.

Lemon Pudding

Makes 3 cups

Blend in a blender until smooth and creamy:

1 lb. tofu	**1/8 tsp. salt**
1/4 cup oil	**6 Tbsp. lemon juice**
2/3 cup sugar	**1/2 tsp. vanilla**

Pour into individual serving dishes or baked pie shell. Chill until set and serve.

Per 1/2 Cup Serving: Calories: 218, Protein: 6 gm., Fat: 12 gm., Carbohydrates: 24 gm.

Strawberry Pudding

Makes 3 1/2 cups

Blend in a blender until smooth and creamy:

1 1/2 cups tofu	**1 1/2 cups fresh ripe strawberries, sliced**
1/3 cup oil	**1 tsp. vanilla**
1/2 cup sugar	**1 Tbsp. lemon juice**
1/4 tsp. salt	

Pour into individual serving dishes or baked pie shell, then chill overnight.

Per 1/2 Cup Serving: Calories: 270, Protein: 6 gm., Fat: 18 gm., Carbohydrates: 26 gm.

Carob Honey Pudding, Strawberry Pudding and Orange Pudding

TOFU TOPPINGS

Serve Tofu Toppings as you would whipped cream. Use only very fresh softer tofu for these toppings and blend them very creamy. Read "Blending Tofu" on p. 7. If you are trying to reduce calories, you can omit the oil from these recipes, which will only slightly change their texture. Serve Tofu Toppings well chilled.

Sweet and Creamy Topping

Makes 1 1/2 cups

Blend in a blender until smooth and creamy:
   1/2 lb. tofu
   1/2 cup oil
   1/4 cup confectioners sugar
   1/2 tsp. lemon juice
   1/8 tsp. salt
Chill and serve as you would whipped cream.

Per 1/4 Cup Serving: Calories: 208, Protein: 3 gm., Fat: 20 gm., Carbohydrates: 6 gm.

Sweet and Creamy Topping With Honey

Makes 1 1/2 cups

Blend in a blender until smooth and creamy:
   1/2 lb. soft tofu
   1/2 Tbsp. lemon juice
   1/4 cup oil
   2 Tbsp. honey
   1/2 tsp. vanilla
   1/4 tsp. salt

Chill and serve as you would whipped cream.

Per 1/4 Cup Serving: Calories: 129, Protein: 3 gm., Fat: 11 gm., Carbohydrates: 7 gm.

TOFU CAKES

Adding tofu to cakes makes a moist cake along with giving a higher protein level. Softer tofu is best for cakes. For successful Tofu Cakes, follow the directions exactly. Put your cake in a preheated oven immediately after mixing the wet and dry ingredients together. Be sure to bake at exactly the temperature specified.

Blueberry Lemon Cake

Serves 12-14
Makes one 10" tube or bundt pan

Preheat oven to 350° F.

Have ready:
**1 (15 oz.) can blueberries, drained or
1 cup fresh blueberries, drained**

Blend in a blender until smooth and creamy:
**1/2 lb. tofu
1/2 cup fresh lemon juice
1/4 cup oil**

Set aside.

Sift together into a bowl:
**2 1/2 cups unbleached white flour
1 1/2 tsp. baking soda
1 tsp. salt**

Stir in:
**3/4 cup water
1/3 cup oil**

Add the tofu mixture and beat 300 strokes or 2-3 minutes with an electric mixer. Gently fold in blueberries. Pour into a well-oiled 10" tube or bundt pan. Bake for 35-45 minutes. When the cake is cooled and turned out of the pan onto a serving platter, glaze with Lemon Glaze, below.

Lemon Glaze

Mix together:
**1 1/2 cups confectioners sugar
1/4 cup fresh lemon juice**

Pour over the top of the cooled cake.

Per Serving: Calories: 277, Protein: 4 gm., Fat: 12 gm., Carbohydrates: 39 gm.

Blueberry Lemon Cake and Carrot Cake

Creme-Filled Crumb Cake

Serves 12
Makes one 10" tube pan

Preheat oven to 375° F.

Use 3 separate bowls to make the 3 separate layers.

First layer

Mix together until crumbly:
- 1/2 cup brown sugar
- 1 cup unbleached white flour
- 1/2 tsp. salt
- 1/2 cup walnuts, chopped
- 1/4 cup oil

Press this mixture into the bottom and sides of the pan.

Second layer

In a blender, blend until smooth and creamy:
- 1 lb. tofu, crumbled
- 3 Tbsp. oil
- 1/2 cup sugar
- 1 Tbsp. vanilla
- 2 Tbsp. unbleached white flour
- 1/2 tsp. salt

Spread on top of the first layer in the pan.

Third layer

In a blender, blend until smooth and creamy:
- 1/2 lb. tofu, crumbled
- 3 Tbsp. fresh lemon juice
- 1/2 cup oil
- 1/2 tsp. salt
- 1 cup sugar
- 3/4 cup water

Mix together in a bowl:
- 2 cups unbleached white flour
- 1/2 tsp. soda
- 2 tsp. baking powder
- 1/2 cup walnuts, chopped
- 1/2 tsp. cinnamon

Stir blended ingredients for third layer into the flour mixture until there are no lumps. Spread this over the second layer, being careful not to stir the second and third layers together. Bake for 40-45 minutes. Let sit for 5 minutes, then loosen the edges and turn out onto a plate or platter. Let it cool 10 minutes before slicing.

Per Serving: Calories: 431, Protein: 8 gm., Fat: 21 gm., Carbohydrates: 53 gm.

Shortcake

Serves 6
Makes twelve 3" cakes

Preheat oven to 400° F.

Mix together in a bowl:
    2 cups unbleached white flour   **1/2 tsp. salt**
    2 tsp. baking powder   **1/3 cup sugar**

Cut in:
    1/3 cup oil

Set aside.

Blend in a blender until smooth and creamy:
    1/2 cup tofu
    3/4 cup water

Mix well with dry ingredients, stirring until it is a smooth dough. Roll out 1/4" thick. Cut with a 3" biscuit cutter. Place half the circles on an oiled cookie sheet.

Oil the top of each with:
    1 tsp. oil

Place another circle on top of each oiled one. Bake for 15 minutes.

When shortcakes are cool, split each one apart and spoon in Sweet and Creamy Topping, p. 145, and then spoon on fresh fruit. Put on the top half of the shortcake and spoon on more topping and fruit.

Per Serving: Calories: 411, Protein: 6 gm., Fat: 23 gm., Carbohydrates: 44 gm.

Chocolate Pudding Cake

Serves 9
Makes one 9" square pan

Preheat oven to 350° F.

Sift together:
    1 1/4 cups unbleached white flour   **1/4 tsp. salt**
    3/4 cup sugar   **1/4 cup cocoa**
    1 1/2 tsp. baking powder

Beat in:
    3/4 cup tofu, crumbled small   **3 Tbsp. oil**
    2/3 cup water   **1/2 cup walnuts or pecans**
    1 tsp. vanilla

Pour into oiled pan.

Mix together:
    2 Tbsp. cocoa
    1 cup sugar

Sprinkle over the top of the batter in the pan, then pour on 1 cup boiling water. Bake for 45 minutes. Serve hot or cold.

Per Serving: Calories: 285, Protein: 5 gm., Fat: 11 gm., Carbohydrates: 45 gm.

Carrot Cake

This recipe is pictured on p. 147.

Serves 12-16
Makes one 9" x 13" pan or
one 9" spring form tube pan

Preheat oven to 350° F.

Mix together dry ingredients:
3 cup unbleached white flour
2 tsp. baking powder
1 tsp. baking soda
1 tsp. cinnamon
1 tsp. salt

Mix well in a separate bowl:
1/2 lb. tofu, blended until smooth
1 lb. carrots, grated (4 1/2-5 cups)
3/4 cup oil
2 cups light brown sugar
1 Tbsp. vanilla
1/4 cup orange juice concentrate

Add dry ingredients to the wet ones. Stir until all dry parts are moistened.

Fold in:
3/4 cup walnuts, chopped
3/4 cup raisins

Oil and flour pan. Bake for 45 minutes. When cool, top with Creamy Glaze Topping, below.

Creamy Glaze Topping

Blend in a blender until smooth and creamy:
1/2 lb. tofu   **3 Tbsp. honey**
1 Tbsp. oil   **1/4 tsp. salt**
1 Tbsp. lemon juice

Per Serving: Calories: 462, Protein: 7 gm., Fat: 18 gm., Carbohydrates: 70 gm.

Peanut Butter Cake

Serves 12
Makes one 9" x 13" cake or two 9" rounds

Preheat oven to 375° F.

Blend in a blender until smooth and creamy:
  1/2 lb. tofu
  1 cup peanut butter
  1/2 cup oil
  1 Tbsp. vanilla
  3/4 cup water
  1 1/2 cups sugar

Set aside.

In a large mixing bowl combine:
  2 1/2 cups unbleached white flour
  2 tsp. baking powder
  1 1/2 tsp. salt
  1/4 tsp. baking soda

Pour the blended mixture into the dry ingredients and mix all together. Oil and flour the baking pans and pour in the batter. Bake for 35 minutes. When cool, frost with Fudge Frosting, below.

Per Serving: Calories: 430, Protein: 10 gm., Fat: 22 gm., Carbohydrates: 50 gm.

Fudge Frosting

Makes 3 cups frosting

Bring to a boil in a heavy-bottomed saucepan:
  2 cups sugar
  1 1/3 cups milk or soymilk
  1/2 tsp. salt

Simmer 10-12 minutes, then remove from heat and add:
  4 (1 oz.) squares unsweetened chocolate

Stir until melted, then cool 15 minutes.

Blend together in a blender:
  1 1/4 cups tofu
  2 Tbsp. oil
  1 Tbsp. vanilla

Beat the blended mixture into the cooled chocolate mixture until thick and creamy, then spread on cake. Allow it to set well before slicing. Can be refrigerated or frozen. This makes enough frosting for one 9" x 13" or two 9" round pans.

Per 1/4 Cup Serving: Calories: 230, Protein: 4 gm., Fat: 10 gm., Carbohydrates: 38 gm.

TOFU ICE CREAM

Tofu Ice Cream has its own unique creamy texture. Serve it as you would any ice cream—in a bowl, on pie a la mode, or in a banana split. Try it also between graham crackers and refrozen as a sandwich, or spread in a prebaked pie shell and refrozen.

Strawberry Tofu Ice Cream
Makes 12 1/2 cups

Blend in a blender in four equal parts until smooth and creamy:

- 2 lbs. soft tofu
- 1 cup milk or soymilk
- 2 cups sugar
- 1 1/3 cups oil
- 1/4 cup fresh lemon juice
- 2 (20 oz.) pkgs. frozen unsweetened strawberries
- 2 Tbsp. vanilla
- 1/4 tsp. salt

Freeze in a home hand-operated or electric ice cream maker and serve.

Per 1/2 Cup Serving: Calories: 204, Protein: 3 gm., Fat: 14 gm., Carbohydrates: 20 gm.

Pineapple Tofu Ice Cream
Makes 13 cups

Blend in a blender in four equal parts until smooth and creamy:

- 2 lbs. soft tofu
- 1 1/3 cups milk or soymilk
- 1 1/3 cups oil
- 2 cups sugar
- 1/4 cup fresh lemon juice
- 2 Tbsp. vanilla
- 2 (20 oz.) cans unsweetened crushed pineapple with syrup (reserving 2/3 cup drained pineapple to stir in before freezing)
- 1/4 tsp. salt

Stir in the reserved 2/3 cup drained pineapple. Freeze in a home hand-operated or electric ice cream maker and serve.

Per 1/2 Cup Serving: Calories: 213, Protein: 3 gm., Fat: 13 gm., Carbohydrates: 23 gm.

Carob Honey Tofu Ice Cream
Makes 9 cups

Blend in a blender in four equal parts until smooth and creamy:

- 2 lbs. tofu
- 2 cups milk or soymilk
- 1 cup oil
- 1 cup honey
- 6 Tbsp. carob
- 3 Tbsp. vanilla
- 1/4 tsp. salt

Freeze in a home hand-operated or electric ice cream maker and serve.

Per 1/2 Cup Serving: Calories: 223, Protein: 5 gm., Fat: 15 gm., Carbohydrates: 20 gm.

Pineapple Tofu Ice Cream, Chocolate Tofu Ice Cream, and Strawberry Tofu Ice Cream

Chocolate Tofu Ice Cream

Makes 10 cups

Blend in a blender in four equal parts until smooth and creamy:

2 lbs. soft tofu	**1/2 cup cocoa**
2 cups milk or soymilk	**2 Tbsp. vanilla**
1 cup oil	**1/4 tsp. salt**
2 cups sugar	

Freeze in a home hand-operated or electric ice cream maker and serve.

Per 1/2 Cup Serving: Calories: 224, Protein: 5 gm., Fat: 14 gm., Carbohydrates: 23 gm.

Banana Honey Tofu Ice Cream

Makes 8 cups

Blend in a blender in four equal parts until smooth and creamy:

1 lb. tofu	**2/3 cup honey**
2 cups milk or soymilk	**3 Tbsp. vanilla**
3/4 cup oil	**1/4 tsp. salt**
5 bananas, ripe	

Freeze in a home hand-operated or electric ice cream maker and serve.

Per 1/2 Cup Serving: Calories: 209, Protein: 4 gm., Fat: 13 gm., Carbohydrates: 23 gm.

Peach Tofu Ice Cream

Makes 13 cups

Marinate together in the refrigerator for one hour:
   8 medium peaches, peeled and chopped (about one quart)
   the juice of 2 lemons
   1 cup sugar
Combine with:

3 cups milk or soymilk	**1/4 cup vanilla**
1 1/2 lbs. tofu	**1/2 tsp. salt**
1 1/4 cups sugar	

Blend in a blender in four equal parts until smooth and creamy. Freeze in a home hand-cranked or electric ice cream maker and serve.

Per 1/2 Cup Serving: Calories: 137, Protein: 3 gm., Fat: 2 gm., Carbohydrates: 18 gm.

MAKING TOFU AT HOME

Making tofu at home is easy to do. It takes some time and organization and provides satisfying results. You will need:

- dried soybeans
- a food processor, blender, hand grain mill, or meat grinder
- a 3 or 4 gallon heavy pot or double boiler
- another large pot or bowl
- a large wire whip
- a 2 to 3 foot square piece of nylon mesh or several layers of cheesecloth
- a large wooden paddle or spoon
- a colander
- a ladle
- a 1/2 gallon jug (to fill with water for a weight)

Home-made Tofu

You will also need a curding agent. Any one of the following will do:

- vinegar (5%)
- lemon juice
- Epsom salts
- nigari

We used vinegar for curding the tofu in these pictures. Vinegar and lemon juice are probably the most widely available curding agents. Epsom salts can be found in drugstores, and nigari can be found in health food stores. Nigari is made by removing the sodium and water from sea water, leaving the remaining minerals in crystal form. Different curding agents give different subtle flavors, texture, and yield in amount of curds. Too much solidifier will give the tofu a strong flavor that is not appetizing. Tofu should have a subtle, fresh flavor.

Preparing the Soybeans

Five cups of soybeans makes about 3 1/2 to 4 lbs. of tofu. Start by rinsing and then soaking 5 cups of whole soybeans in 15 cups cold water overnight, or at least 8 to 10 hours. Be sure to keep the soaking beans in a cool place or under refrigeration if the weather is very hot so they won't sour. Soured beans will make thinner milk and therefore less yield. You can quick-soak your beans by pouring 15 cups of boiling water over the rinsed soybeans and letting them soak for 2 to 4 hours. Soybeans will double in size and be free of wrinkles when they are finished soaking. If you split one in half, it will have a flat surface inside, rather than a concave surface.

After the soybeans have been soaked, rinse them in a colander. Now they are ready for grinding. You can use a food processor, grinding 2 cups of soaked soybeans at a time into a slightly gritty or sandy paste. The grinding can also be done in a meat grinder, using the finer grind. If it is ground too smooth it will be hard to strain and the resulting milk will have a pulpy texture. If it is not ground finely enough, it will not give a good yield.

Cooking the Soymilk

Using a large wire whip, whip the soybean paste into about 2 gallons of rapidly boiling water (3 cups boiling water to every cup of soaked beans). Bring it back to a boil, turn down to medium low heat, and let it cook at a low boil for 15 to 20 minutes, stirring occasionally. Watch the pot carefully, because soymilk can foam up and boil over quickly. Keep a cup of cold water next to the pot, to pour in if it starts to foam up quickly.

If you cook on an electric stove, you may have to remove the pot from the burner to adjust the heat if it starts to boil over.

Adding the soybean paste to boiling water

Cooking the soymilk

Blender Method

The grinding can also be done in a blender. For every cup of soaked soybeans, add 3 cups of water to the blender. The water can be either hot or cold. Blend this at high speed into a fine slurry (about one minute), then pour into a heavy pot or double boiler. Bring to a low boil and cook for 15 minutes.

Straining the Soymilk

Set a colander over a large bowl or pot and line the colander with a large piece (about 2 to 3 foot square) of nylon mesh or several layers of cheesecloth. Pour or ladle the cooked soybean mixture into the cloth-lined colander. Gather up two corners of the cloth in each hand and raise the ball of pulp a few inches out of the colander. Roll it back and forth in the cloth by alternately raising and lowering each hand. This will release most of the soymilk. Set the cloth and contents back into the colander, gather up the ends of the cloth again and twist them together until the cloth tightens around the ball of pulp.

Press the bundle with a wooden paddle or a jar to extract as much milk as possible. You can open the cloth up after you have pressed out all the milk, and mix 2 to 3 cups of boiling water into the pulp. Twist the cloth back up and press again. The pulp can be reserved for baking.

Some of the recipes in this book call for soymilk. When making tofu, you can reserve part of the soymilk to use in cooking later. Remember to adjust the amount of curding agent to maintain the correct proportions. Soymilk also makes a tasty, nutritious drink when sweetened, and can be served either hot or chilled.

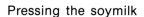

Pressing the soymilk

Adding the curding agent to the soymilk

Finished curds and whey

Curding the Soymilk

Dilute 1/2 cup of vinegar in 1 1/2 cups of hot water. For other curding agents see the table below. For the highest yield of tofu, the curding should be done slowly (in a few stages). This provides large, soft curds and yields a tofu high in water content.

Stir the freshly strained soymilk in a slow circular motion while it is still hot (about 185° F.). Stop the paddle upright to create a turbulence and immediately add 1 1/4 cups of the vinegar solution. Stir the soymilk once in the opposite direction. Sprinkle 1/2 cup of the vinegar solution over the top of the soymilk, cover to retain the heat and let it sit undisturbed for 5 minutes. The soymilk will start to form large white curds. If there is still soymilk present, poke gently to activate curding and gently stir in the remaining 1/4 cup of vinegar solution. Cover the pot again and leave it 2 to 3 more minutes.

The curds are complete when they are surrounded by the clear yellow liquid called *whey*. If a very firm tofu is desired, the curds in the whey may be placed back on the heat and boiled a few minutes.

If there is a lot of whey and only a few curds, the beans may not have been ground finely enough, resulting in thin milk and low yield.

The whey acts as a natural detergent and will suds easily if stirred. It is good for washing and soaking the pots and cloths used during the tofu-making process.

Now the curds are ready to be pressed.

CURDING AGENTS

Soybeans	Warm Water	Curding Agent
1 lb. (2 1/2 cups)	1 cup	1/4 cup vinegar or lemon juice
1 lb. (2 1/2 cups)	1 1/2 cups	1 1/2 to 2 tsp. Nigari or Epsom salts
2 lbs. (5 cups)	1 1/2 cups	1/2 cup vinegar or lemon juice
2 lbs. (5 cups)	2 cups	3 to 4 tsp. Nigari or Epsom salts

Dipping out the whey

Ladling the curds into a cloth-lined colander

Pressing the Tofu

Line your colander or pressing box with a nylon mesh cloth or several layers of cheesecloth and set it up in the sink or over a bowl or pot.

Set the pot of curds and whey next to it. Set a large strainer in the pot to fill with whey, but keep the curds out. Then ladle out whey until most of it is out of the pot. This will help the curds form together into a nice solid tofu.

Next, ladle the curds into the colander or pressing box lined with the cloth.

Fold the cloth tightly around the curds, top with a flat plate and a weight. A half-gallon or gallon jar filled with water makes a good weight, or you can use a clean, heavy rock or brick. Press for 20 to 30 minutes. For firmer tofu use a heavier weight or press for a longer time.

When you remove the weight and the plate and fold back the cloth, the tofu should be firm to the touch. Gently remove the block from the colander or pressing box, and set it in a sink or

bowl of cold water. Remove the cloth and leave the block in the water until it is cool and firm.

Store your tofu in a container of cold water in the refrigerator, changing the water daily to preserve freshness. It will keep this way up to one week.

Care and Maintenance of Equipment

Clean your milk-making equipment and cloth well immediately after each use. A mild soap solution may be used. Cloths can be soaked in bleach water occasionally after washing. A vegetable brush is a good cleaning tool for your colander, press and cloth. For easiest cleaning, soak the pot used for cooking the soymilk in water immediately after emptying. You will probably have to use a copper or stainless steel scrubber on that pot. Keep everything clean as you make your soymilk and tofu. The sooner your utensils are washed or rinsed, the easier they are to clean.

INDEX

Fahrenheit to Centigrade Conversion Chart

Fahrenheit	Centigrade
300°	150°
325°	163°
350°	177°
375°	190°
400°	204°
425°	218°
450°	232°